D0934137

TREVOR BROOKING

TREVOR BROOKING

with the assistance of Brian Scovell

PELHAM BOOKS

First published in Great Britain by
Pelham Books Ltd
44 Bedford Square
London WC1B 3DU
1981

© Trevor Brooking 1981

All Rights Reserved. No part of this publication may be
reproduced, stored in a retrieval system, or transmitted, in any form
or by any means, electronic, mechanical, photocopying,
recording or otherwise, without the prior permission of the
Copyright owner

*Trevor Brooking wishes to express his thanks to the following for permission
to use pictures: Monte Fresco of the* Daily Mirror, *Reg Lancaster of the*
Daily Express, *Arthur Edwards of the* Sun, *Tower Hamlet Studios, PA
Photos, Central Press, Sporting Pictures (UK) Ltd and Steve Bacon.*

British Library Cataloguing in Publication Data
Brooking, Trevor
  Trevor, Brooking.
  1. Soccer players – Great Britain
  – Biography
  I. Title   II. Scovell, Brian
  716.334'0924   GV942.7.B

ISBN 0 7207 1374 9

Photoset by Robcroft Ltd, London WC1
Printed and bound in Great Britain by
Billing & Sons Ltd, Guildford, London and Worcester

Contents

Introduction

by Brian Scovell of the *Daily Mail*

Trevor Brooking is a gentleman in a rough game – an authentic English sporting hero. As football has become fiercer, more competitive and less enjoyable, he has carried on delighting us with his skill. He is one of the few players left in England who can bring people out of their seats in rapt appreciation.

He is an honest player in a sport that can at times be very dishonest. He has never been involved in any scandal. Nobody has accused him of selling his soul or trying to cripple an opponent. He has never been sent off and in a career lasting sixteen years has only been cautioned five times. His record is above reproach. As a player of unique skill in a game that has become over-competitive and over-physical he is ideally placed to talk about what is wrong and how it can be put right. He is the thinking man's footballer.

I must confess there is a personal reason which influenced me when Malcolm Hamer first asked me whether I was interested in helping with Trevor's book. When he was six years old, my son Gavin was asked if he had a hero. 'Trevor Brooking,' he said. That came as a surprise to me because I did not think he had a hero. He had never attended a professional football match and was too young to watch much football on television. Yet Trevor was his idol and West Ham his favourite team.

It was significant, I felt, that when I asked Trevor if he had a hero he replied: 'Bobby Charlton.' Charlton was the gentleman footballer of the 1960s, a household name in almost every country of the world. Everyone needs a hero to look up to and I am pleased that I have had this opportunity of collaborating with one of the few left in the modern game.

Bromley, Kent
May 1981

1

Promotion

When I look back over my sixteen years as a professional footballer I think of many things, most of them pleasurable. I started in the First Division and in a few years time I hope to finish my career in the First Division with the same club – West Ham. In an unstable industry I have been lucky enough to find stability and order.

In those sixteen years standards have declined and there are fewer skilled players in the game than when I started as an apprentice on 24 July 1965. Football has become more a business and less a sport. Players have become more regimented but I am lucky to have worked under two managers who value skill and who have allowed me to express whatever skill I possess. Ron Greenwood, who launched my career in the West Ham first team against the Swiss club Grasshoppers in June 1966, is perhaps the leading advocate of the school of thought that believes in letting good players play. And John Lyall, who succeeded him at Upton Park in September 1974, is a firm believer in that same creed.

Unlike many footballers, I completed my education before I established myself in the West Ham side at the age of twenty-two. If I failed to make the grade I had something to fall back on. So many players leave football clubs at an early age and are never heard of again. The wastage rate in football is high and it is getting higher as the industry contracts. When I started at Upton Park there were about fifty professionals at the club. Now there are half that number and there is no longer an 'A' team.

With the game in its present economic state, this process of reduction will continue and it will be harder, not easier, to make a career in football. In the summer of 1980 there was an unprecedented number of players given free transfers and many were unable to find clubs. I can foresee, in the not too distant future, a time when many Third and Fourth Division clubs will employ part-time players who have another job outside football. The wealthier First and Second Division clubs will have to make cuts as well, carrying only a first team squad of seventeen or eighteen players.

The most significant development in my time is the way the game has become big business with inflation inside football outstripping inflation in ordinary life. The highest transfer fees paid out in 1966 (the year I was signed as a full professional) were all under £100,000 and the players transferred were quality players like Frank McLintock and Terry Venables, who both cost £80,000, Charlie Cooke, Alan Gilzean and Alan Mullery, who cost £72,000 each, and Joe Baker at £65,000.

Nowadays, the top fees approach £1·5m and although there were signs in 1980-81 that fees were levelling out, the madness is still there. It has to be crazy when a club pays out more on one player than it receives through the gate in a single season. The galloping inflation exists in other areas. Players' wages are proportionately higher, although I do not subscribe to the view that most professionals are overpaid. The receipts from the 1966 FA Cup Final totalled £109,691. The receipts from the 1980 Cup Final when I headed the only goal against Arsenal which was the highlight of my career, came to £729,000 or in other words nearly seven times as much.

In those sixteen years I have seen a sad decline in standards among supporters attending matches. My father used to take me to see West Ham's home games and we stood on the North Bank just to the right of the goal. This would not be possible today. There are too many unruly and undisciplined young people attending football matches these days and they have contributed most to the decline in attendances. Measures taken by the police have kept hooliganism relatively under control inside grounds but the problem will remain until standards of behaviour generally start improving.

Players themselves have a responsibility. I believe that we

have allowed ourselves to be caught up in the over-competitiveness of the game. There is too much 'kidology', too many instances of players diving in the penalty area to claim a penalty so that when there is a foul the referee has a hard job deciding whether one has actually been committed. The referee has a much harder task than Jack Taylor had when he refereed that 1966 FA Cup Final between Everton and Sheffield Wednesday.

In my early days when a player went down injured an opposing player would kick the ball into touch, but nowadays play will often continue. Although many managers now fine their players for arguing with referees, there is still too much of it going on. I have been guilty of it myself. It is caused by pressure and there is certainly more pressure in the game today than there has ever been.

The 1980-81 season was probably my most successful because West Ham reached the final of the League Cup, achieved promotion from the Second Division and reached the quarter finals of the European Cup Winners Cup. But during that season I was cautioned twice whereas in the previous eleven years I had been booked on only three occasions.

I could have been sent off in the League Cup Final against Liverpool at Wembley on 14 March 1981. That was the 'interfering with play' Final when FIFA referee Clive Thomas allowed Alan Kennedy's goal to stand near the end, although his shot had passed over the head of the recumbent Sammy Lee who was in an offside position. Phil Parkes said afterwards that Sammy had to duck otherwise the ball would have hit him. 'It had to be a case of him interfering with play,' said Phil.

We protested so volubly that we persuaded Clive to go over and see the linesman who had raised his flag for offside. He was still some yards away from the linesman when he said: 'I am over-ruling you because he wasn't interfering with play.' Later he admitted that this was bad refereeing and he should have gone up to the linesman and talked with him. The linesman might have pointed out that Lee was in a much more incriminating position than Colin Irwin had been when Thomas disallowed a Lee 'goal' earlier on. I thought we were lucky to get away with that because Irwin was wide of the goal and not interfering with play.

Thomas had previously had a reputation for ruling out goals when a player was interfering with play. Now we had a case of him being inconsistent. Irwin, who was away from the line of the ball, was offside whereas Lee, who was under the path of Kennedy's shot, was not. It is a law that is always open to controversy because it depends on who is refereeing the particular match and how he interprets the law. What I could not accept in the League Cup final was the referee interpreting the law two different ways in the same match. In the 1977-78 season when West Ham went down, there were two similar decisions which went against us and probably cost us our place in the First Division with all that meant in bonuses and extra status.

As West Ham's players continued to argue with Thomas at Wembley, he strode off saying: 'That's it, I've given a goal.' If it had happened earlier in the game we would not have been so worked up and would have had a chance to get ourselves back into the game. But there was so little time left. After holding the Football League champions for so long we thought we were going out on a disputed decision.

Once play resumed, Ray Stewart fouled Ray Kennedy and Thomas blew for a foul. I was close by and said: 'That's the result of the frustration from that decision thirty seconds ago.' I did not swear and I did not say it insultingly. But in the circumstances it was totally wrong of me to get involved. Clive was very snappy. 'I don't need you to tell me my job,' he said. Normally he is a referee a player can talk to during a game and I thought my opinion was fair comment, but he started to get his book out and said: 'I am booking you as well.'

In our next attack Alan Devonshire was brought down on the edge of the area and we were awarded a free kick. I said: 'Is it direct or indirect?' He pointed at the ball and said: 'What's it doing here?' He felt I was implying, perhaps, that it should have been a penalty.

'All I want to know is whether it is direct or indirect,' I said. 'I haven't given a signal, have I?' he said. 'It's direct.' Referees have to raise an arm when it is an indirect free kick but some raise it and put it down again and it is not always clear to the players.

I realised he was so testy that if I persisted I might go off so I said nothing more. It was the closest I had ever been to being sent off a football field. From the free kick Ray Clemence made a fantastic save to deny Ray Stewart the equaliser. Jimmy Neighbour took the corner, Alvin Martin headed for Clemence's top left-hand corner and the ball would have gone in if Terry McDermott had not pushed it over the bar – so cleverly that I am sure some people did not think it was a hand ball.

Fortunately, Clive saw it and awarded a penalty. The pressure on Ray Stewart was immense and I would certainly not have liked to take it myself. As he prepared to address the ball, I noticed a Liverpool player motioning Clemence to his right which is the usual side Stewart puts his penalties. I thought Ray would blast it. He usually does. Instead he sidefooted the ball in the other side for one of the coolest pieces of penalty taking under stress that I have ever seen. There was no time to restart the game. Clive Thomas blew the final whistle and we started to go towards the Royal Box in a state of confusion. When there is no presentation to the winners players do not know what to do. There was similar confusion in the FA Cup Final between Spurs and Manchester City a few weeks later, when everyone, including supporters, had a feeling of anti-climax.

The first I knew of the much-publicised altercation between John Lyall and Clive Thomas was when I heard David Cross say to John: 'Don't get involved, John.' I didn't hear what John was saying to Thomas or what Thomas said to him, but both men looked agitated. Apparently, Thomas made the initial approach, possibly seeking to explain the disallowed goal, but John revealed he had said: 'I don't want to talk about it. We feel we have been cheated.'

Thomas's comment afterwards was: 'No-one calls me a cheat. I am reporting the matter to the Football Association.' It was very uncharacteristic of John because he never gets involved in rows. Some managers stoke up controversy but he always tries to play it down.

The FA charged him with insulting behaviour, not the

customary charge of 'bringing the game into disrepute', and when the case was heard he was absolved of any blame. He left the FA commission without a stain on his character and the players were delighted with the result. During twenty-five years in the game this was the first time John had appeared at an FA hearing. His record was above reproach – and still is.

When I saw the TV version of the match the next day it confirmed what I had felt at the time. Clive Thomas had made a mistake but it didn't matter so much as we thought it would at the time because we earned a replay. Neither side had really deserved to win. After conceding the first half we played ourselves back into it by patiently building up our attacks from the back. John thought that presented the best chance of beating Liverpool by denying them possession.

In the replay at Villa Park on Wednesday 1 April we had little opportunity to take possession of the ball in the first half. Liverpool played as well as I had ever seen them for forty-five minutes and annihilated us. Kenny Dalglish gave a superb exhibition of centre-forward play and the goal he volleyed from Terry McDermott's lobbed pass was the kind of instinctive goal that only he could score.

The second goal in their 2-1 victory was lucky. Alan Hansen's header would probably have been stopped by Phil Parkes but it struck Billy Bonds and flew into the roof of the net. Clive Thomas was again the referee and the West Ham fans booed him for much of the first half. I felt that he was doing his best to stay out of the limelight, sometimes letting incidents go unpunished to allow the game to flow.

I thought the free kick which led to Ian Rush hitting the bar was taken when the ball was moving and it was also unfair on us because Thomas had barely finished lecturing Billy who was consequently out of position. People said afterwards that I looked tired on television but my retort was: 'So would you after being given a run around like that in the first half!' It is always more exhausting when the other team have the ball all the time and you have to run after them. If your team has it, you can do just as much running but not feel so tired.

In the game Liverpool always seemed to have a man spare which was the hallmark of their great days. They played at tremendous pace and I was pleased to see Phil Neal, who was booed the week before by the Wembley crowd during the international against Spain, have the kind of game which silenced his critics.

Jimmy Neighbour, who scored the late goal against Coventry in the second leg semi-final which earned us our chance in the Final, also had a commanding match which pleased us because he is such a popular player. It was his run up the right and well-struck cross which Paul Goddard headed in for our goal at Villa Park.

Liverpool thoroughly deserved their first League Cup success despite the fact that we came back into the game after the interval and could indeed have won it. Paul Goddard put me through but my shot swerved wide of the far post. Billy Bonds headed over when Alvin Martin was standing behind him and might have done better with it and Clemence made a fine left-handed diving save from Dave Cross's shot.

It had been a highly entertaining game on a peculiar pitch. The groundstaff had covered the central areas which were hard and slightly on the bumpy side. But the wings were soft and yielding so players really needed to wear two types of boots – longer studs for the flanks and shorter studs for the middle of the pitch.

The League Cup losers' medal brought my total of medals in my career to five. That may not seem much but many notable players go through their careers without a single medal. When I was a schoolboy player I seemed to be winning medals and trophies every season and the sideboard was full of them! But in the professional game there are ninety-two starters and only six winners in domestic football. Often the same clubs win the prizes. My most cherished medals are the FA Cup winners' medals I won in 1975 and 1980. I keep them in the safe at my bank because I have heard too many stories of players having them stolen or mislaid. Bob Wilson, the former Arsenal goalkeeper and BBC TV presenter, had his stolen but as it was insured the FA issued him with a replacement.

An FA Cup Final winners' medal costs £210 plus VAT to make and is made by the Birmingham company which made the first medals for the inaugural Cup Final in 1872, Fattorini and

Son. It is made of nine carat gold and is simply inscribed: 'The FA Challenge Cup Winners.' There is no date, no name and if the recipient wants his name on it he has to pay for it to be inscribed himself.

The League Cup winners medal, which is much less impressive, is also made by a Birmingham company, Vaughtons. Three days after the Liverpool replay I qualified for another medal when West Ham beat Bristol Rovers 2-0 and regained their position in the First Division. We had champagne in the dressing room but most of our fans had gone home before the results of the other games came through and confirmed that we were up.

The real celebration took place after the last home match against Wrexham on 21 May 1981 when we clinched the Second Division championship by a margin of thirteen points. Our campaign had started badly the previous August with a 1-2 home defeat at the hands of Luton Town but a 4-0 victory over Notts County at the end of the month saw us on our way. Christmas was the crucial time. We went to QPR on Boxing Day and were outplayed 3-0 by Terry Venables's side. The omens were not so good but we attributed it to over-indulging on Christmas Day. Normally footballers have to report to a hotel after lunch on Christmas Day to prepare for the next day's match. I do not think West Ham will allow us that licence in future years!

We beat Orient at home the next day and disappointingly went out of the FA Cup in the Third round in a second replay against Wrexham. Maybe that was just as well because it saved us from the kind of fixture congestion which overloaded Ipswich Town's season. The most crucial victory of our season was at Swansea City on 10 January 1981. John Toshack had transformed City into promotion candidates yet we defeated them 3-1 and stayed well in front of the field for the rest of the season.

My Second Division championship medal joined my two FA Cup winners' medals, my League Cup losers' medal and my European Cup Winners Cup Final losers' medal from 1976. However, more valued than the medals, the many England caps I have earned and the money, is the personal satisfaction I have gained from being lucky enough to be given the chance to enjoy a life that is envied by millions of people. If I have been critical of certain aspects of the game – the decline in standards, hooliganism and over-commercialism – it is because I care deeply about football and want to see it maintain its position as the country's national sport. We hold it in trust for the next generation.

2

Beginnings

I was born at one o'clock in the afternoon at Barking Maternity Hospital on 2 October, 1948, and I weighed eight pounds eleven ounces, slightly above average weight. My parents, Henry Charles Brooking (Harry to everyone including me) and Margaret Ethel, liked the name Trevor because they knew someone at work with that name. My mother wanted my second name to be Alan until the midwife pointed out that my initials would then be TAB. So my parents settled on David although we have no Welsh links in the family.

My parents both come from the East End of London, where they still live. They met in their teens while working at a Co-op store. My father left to enter the Metropolitan Police Force and retired as a sergeant after serving twenty-six years. My brother Tony followed him into the police and is now an inspector. During the Blitz, my father was at a police station one night when a bomb fell on a nearby pub. A fireman rushed in and asked him to help at the fire which resulted. But as they returned to the scene another bomb landed nearby killing six people, including the fireman and severely injuring my father who was the only survivor. He was rushed to hospital and had several operations to remove fragments of glass from his head. For several days he could not recognize anyone, and there were fears that he might not be the same person again.

Fortunately he soon recovered although bits of glass kept coming out of his head for some time afterwards. It is now a joke in our family, the time dad went off his head. After leaving the police force, he worked as a school attendance officer for the Greater London Council and retired at Christmas 1980. When

Tony was born my mother stopped working in the Co-op, and to bring in extra cash she used to make Christmas crackers at home.

My first school was Ripple School which I attended until I was eleven. It was about fifteen minutes walk from where we lived in Barking and I used to run along the pavement kicking a tennis ball against the garden fences, controlling the rebound. Time after time I would repeat this and I think this early training may account for why I am looked on as a fairly skilful player.

My father was an aggressive centre-half in a local police side and from a very early age he used to have Tony and me in the garden practising with both feet. He would throw the ball at our 'bad' foot, my left, for hours at a time until we became equally adept at using both feet. I first remember him doing this when I was four and at that age, it is easier to adopt good habits.

I think this was the key factor in my footballing ability. Not many professionals are two-footed – I would say less than a quarter – and those that are have a tremendous advantage. I am generally thought of as a left-footed player because I have played on the left on many occasions, particularly for England. But my 'true' foot, the one I kicked with first when I was a toddler in the garden, is my right. Most of the great players are two-footed, and Bobby Charlton and Johan Cruyff are perhaps the outstanding examples. Ray Wilkins of Manchester United and Glenn Hoddle of Tottenham Hotspur in the current England squad are both two-footed and benefit enormously from it. Defenders can block opponents if they know which way they are going to go but they cannot pre-judge when a player is capable of taking the ball with either foot.

Of course there are notable exceptions. The Hungarian, Ferenc Puskas, was basically a one-footed player, but he had one of the best left foots in the history of the game. In domestic English football Arnold Muhren, the Holland international who plays for Ipswich, is predominantly left-footed and this has not impaired his effectiveness. Frans Thijssen, his Dutch colleague, is stronger with his right foot and so is Osvaldo Ardiles of Tottenham Hotspur. Both of these players have made important contributions to British football. Not many defenders can tackle equally well with both feet. They usually prefer to go in on one side and if their opponent knows that, it is easier for him to attack their weak side. Perhaps the leading two-footed tackler is the Ipswich captain Mick Mills, a fine all-round player whose consistency has been remarkable. He rarely misses a game.

The Brooking family has always been a happy family. My parents made sure we maintained certain standards, but they were not over-strict. I think many of our friends were in awe of us as a family because my father was a policeman. I cannot remember having any fights with Tony because he was six foot three and I wasn't too optimistic about the outcome. He was shy in those days, but being three-and-a-half years older, I looked up to him and went everywhere with him. His friends and I used to climb over a fence at the South East Essex Technical College – it had spikes on top of it I remember – to play football in the grounds. The caretaker's house was on the other side, but when we saw him coming we would climb back over the fence and run home.

This Upton Park of ours was called 'The Field' and we played there for hours each day until it became dark. As most of the other boys were Tony's age, I was the youngest in the group and they called me 'Little 'Un' although I was quite big for my age. We played so often that the ground became churned up and I think this early practice on such a surface made me into a better player on a muddy pitch.

Tony and I always had a Frido plastic football and our friends would knock at the door and ask if we could come out to play soccer with them. We were often the only kids who had a ball. If it was punctured on the spikes, which frequently happened, we had to seal it with an improvised soldering kit.

I was eight when I was first recognized as a potential footballer. One of the teachers at Ripple School, Mr Clarke, saw me playing with a tennis ball in the playground and called me over.

'Have you got any boots?' he asked.

Tony and I always had boots but mine were at home.

'Run home and get them,' said the teacher. 'I want you to play in a school trial this afternoon.'

I must have impressed him because I was selected for the next school match. We were 2-1 in the lead when the referee awarded us a penalty. I was one of the youngest players on the pitch and the one with the least experience, but I put my hand up and said: 'Please Sir, can I take it?'

Such confidence from a newcomer was unknown but the teacher must have liked my self confidence – penalty taking is all about confidence – and allowed me to take it. I strolled up nonchalantly to the ball and scored easily. At that age you do not think about it. But when I was fifteen I was asked to take a penalty while playing for Essex Schools against London Schools in a match at Upton Park and the tension was too much for me. I missed it. We lost the match and that was the last penalty I ever took.

My childhood was in the early days of television. We had a small black and white set, but I have never been a compulsive TV watcher. I rarely see more than half a dozen programmes a week now. At school I was not a natural at studying and had to work hard, although I never found having to sit down and do my homework an unpleasant exercise. I did not have many girl-friends and Tony and I spent most of our time reliving the actions of our sporting heroes. Mine was Bobby Charlton. Besides football, we also used to stage our own Wimbledon and our own mini-Olympics.

I passed the eleven plus examination to Ilford County High School, a grammar school about an hour's bus ride and walk away. We were never taken to school by car in those days. John Lyall, later to become my manager at West Ham, had been a pupil there. It was a good school with excellent standards. The cane was used but I cannot remember having been given it. I had my hair pulled a few times by the English teacher for talking and this might explain why when I took my first batch of GCEs, I failed in English Language. There was little indiscipline in those days and there was no hooliganism at football matches. I believe that the two are linked today. As discipline has deteriorated in the home and in the schools, so hooliganism has mushroomed in our national game.

I was ten when my father first took me to a match at Upton Park. We stood on the North Bank surrounded by fathers and sons who felt safe, without the need to be protected by police. In matches where there was a crush, the boys would be passed down to the front over the heads of the adult spectators. There was a friendly atmosphere and a tingling of excitement that would sustain you to the next home game. Liverpool were the opponents on my very first visit during West Ham's promotion season of 1958 and they were leading 1-0 until John Bond levelled the score with one of his special thirty-yard shots.

I regularly attended home games on Saturdays until my footballing commitments at school and district level stopped me going. But my father continued to take me to mid-week matches. If I had a son of that age today I doubt whether I would let him stand on the terraces. It is sad, these are no longer safe places and this will not change until discipline returns to our society.

I am not an advocate of corporal punishment but the cane will have to be used again in schools if this trend is to be reversed. Since passing my FA Coaching Full Badge, I have taken sessions at a number of schools in the East End and have been appalled by the standard of behaviour. Respect for authority seems to have disappeared and it must be very hard for teachers to do their work in such an environment. Boys were rude and disinterested in their studies and football was about the only part of their lives they showed much interest in. The noise and back-chat in classes stop those children who want to work from benefiting from their lessons. My experiences in business have convinced me that this virtual breakdown in discipline at some schools has a bearing on the unemployment situation with young people. Several times I have interviewed boys who were applying for jobs and they were unable to read properly or add up. Their time at school had been wasted.

These young people would experience a severe shock if they had to submit to the discipline of professional football. Old fashioned disciplines still apply at most Football League clubs and if a young apprentice shows a lack of respect for someone in authority he would soon be made to regret it. He would have to do extra training or, if that failed, he would be fined. The ultimate deterrent is the sack and the end of what might have been a promising career.

I wonder too whether soccer 'hooligans' could be asked to carry out different types of community service where they might start to appreciate that they are not so badly off. I have a fairly close connection with a residential centre in Essex called New Mossford which caters for almost seventy handicapped children between the ages of four and eighteen. The friendliness and vitality of these children, and many youngsters like them, would I am sure be food for thought for some of our more unruly element.

I believe players have a responsibility to behave and set examples, but I do not subscribe to the view that what happens on the field is a direct cause of trouble off of it. There has been one proven case where an incident on the field has caused a riot – the Terry Curran-Simon Stainrod clash at Oldham in the 1980-81 season – but that was very much an exception.

The worst match incident I have been involved in was at Newcastle in 1979 when a petrol bomb was thrown into the crowd. I was bending down to place the ball for a corner when I saw a flash behind me. I did not know what had happened until after the match, but luckily the incident did not lead to a riot as it could well have done. I heard later that the offender received a prison sentence.

As I was tall for my age, I was selected as a wing-half when I was chosen for the district under-thirteen side while at Ilford County High School, but was soon switched to right-back. That upset my father who used to watch the matches and after a short spell as a striker, I reverted to midfield where I have been ever since. I was picked for Ilford Schools to play for the English Schools Trophy and we had a good run before being knocked out by Oxford Schools. By this time I was playing for London and Essex Schools and the professional scouts were taking an interest in me. I was chosen for England Schools in the 1963-64 season as a right-half, but George Luke, the former Newcastle and Chelsea player whose career was virtually ended by a car crash, was preferred in that position when the first match against West Germany was played that season at Wembley. I came in for the second game against the Germans at Middlesbrough's Ayresome Park and it was not a particularly distinguished début. I was kept in the squad for the home internationals but failed to make another appearance. I was looking forward to a trip to Belfast to play Northern Ireland only to learn that the squad of sixteen had been reduced to fifteen, and I was the one to be left out. I was very upset at my first real taste of the ups and downs of football.

At fifteen I was jogging along in the fourth year at school when it occurred to me that I would soon have to make a decision about my future career. If I had continued at school, I suppose I would have eventually become an accountant. My parents were anxious for me to gain some more qualifications, English Language for example, but the pressure from football was building up. Dick Walker, the Spurs scout, had been to see me and so had Jimmy Thompson of Chelsea. I had been training with both clubs but had not made a decision about which one to join. West Ham, whom I supported and had grown up with, was the other club to take an interest in me. Ron Greenwood had watched me in some of the schools' games with his scout Wally St Pier and was prepared to let me continue my studies for a further year. Chelsea and Spurs wanted me to sign as an apprentice immediately.

West Ham did not offer my parents any money, but I have to confess that one club offered them £500 and a car. The offer was promptly rejected. Tommy Docherty, then the Chelsea manager, impressed us as a man prepared to take a lot of trouble to sign what he thought was a promising young player. He sent us four complimentary tickets for the West Ham v Preston FA Cup Final of 1964, but as West Ham had offered us two – which we paid for – my father returned them.

West Ham's willingness to let me carry on with my studies, plus my childhood allegiance to them, meant there was no real decision about which club I should join. West Ham was my club: I could not turn them down. I signed as an apprentice on 24 July 1965. By that time I had gained most of my 'O' Levels although I continued day classes. I passed eleven 'O' Levels and Economics and Accounts at 'A' Level. So many young footballers fail to make the grade that I felt it was vital to have some qualifications behind me.

3

Début

I had a frightening illustration of the uncertainty of professional football as a career in my very first week as an apprentice at West Ham. When the players reported back for training at Chadwell Heath, a press day was held for the photographers to take their stock pictures. Two months earlier West Ham had won the European Cup Winners Cup beating TSV Munich 1860 2-0 at Wembley and both goals had been scored by Alan Sealey. Known as 'Sammy the seal', Sealey was a chirpy mickey-taker who had not quite made it at the highest level until that wonderful day at Wembley. Being the match winner had done a lot for his confidence and he started the 1965-66 season expecting to be challenging for a regular place in the side. The previous season he had played only half of West Ham's League matches and scored two goals. But 'Sammy' was not going to be given a chance to become a star. Near one of the training pitches there were some forms for the players to sit on during a team photographic session, and while playing cricket and larking about he ran straight into one and broke his leg. He was in the field and someone had hit a skier. West Ham had a number of good cricketers on the staff at the time including Geoff Hurst, who had played at quite a high standard, Jim Standen and Bobby Moore. Sealey started running for the catch, eyes on the ball. Some of the other players tried to warn him that he was running into trouble, but in the general hubbub he failed to hear their shouts. It was a sickening reminder to a young player that football is a very fickle occupation and that your dreams could soon be shattered. Alan Sealey was never the same player when he returned later in the season.

I was overawed by all the great names round me as Ron Greenwood introduced me on my first day. Bobby Moore, who was at his peak at this time, shook hands and wished me well. In his brief speech, Ron said he hoped I would stay with the club many years. He was right about that. Only Frank Lampard, who arrived at the same time, and myself, still survive as players, although John Lyall, who was then working in the wages department and helping out with the youth team coaching, had not long retired.

Eight apprentices joined in 1965 and it was a good intake because most of them stayed on to make a career in the game. Too often in football youngsters fail to make the grade and have to find jobs outside the game without having the advantage of an apprenticeship. One of the group was my friend from my Ilford Schools days, Barry Simmons, who was a centre-forward. He is now a taxi driver and out of the game altogether. Another one was Bob Glozier, a full-back who captained England Schools and kept John Craggs, the Middlesbrough and former Newcastle full-back, out of the side the year I played in the team. Bob now works in education and does some coaching. Three others are still connected with the game – Jimmy Lindsay, a Scots inside-forward who went to Shrewsbury, Steve Death, the Reading goalkeeper who is one of the shortest goalkeepers in the Football League, and Roger Cross who was formerly with Brentford and Fulham and is now youth team coach at Millwall. The remaining two are also now out of football, Paul Heffer, a centre-half who played a few first team games, owns two greengrocery shops and David James, a wing-half, lives and works in Southend. West Ham had a good youth side that year and we reached the semi-final of the FA Youth Challenge Cup. We went out of the competition on a 2-3 aggregate score to Birmingham when we felt we had done enough to get through. Birmingham's centre-forward in the two legs was Bob Latchford.

There were some lively characters in the West Ham first team squad at that time, including Cockney wits such as Peter Brabrook, Brian Dear and Johnny 'Budgie' Byrne. 'Budgie' was a delightful fellow whom it was impossible to dislike. He was very undisciplined, particularly when it came to drinking, but whenever Ron Greenwood had him in for a dressing-down it usually ended up with them both bursting out laughing. 'Budgie' would always say something to change the atmosphere. It was difficult to keep a straight face when he was around. On the field, he was the best one touch player I have ever seen. Bobby Moore would find him with a long pass from the back and he would flick it out to Brabrook on the right or John Sissons on the left in one exciting movement. He scored some memorable goals in his time at the club. After West Ham's FA Cup victory over Fulham in 1975, we staged a testimonial match, the 1975 Cup winning side against the 1964 Cup winning side and 'Budgie' came back from South Africa, where he was managing a club, to take part in it. I was astounded when I saw him. He was like a barrel. He became so exhausted after playing in the first half that he had to lie down in the dressing room and rest for the whole of the second half after complaining of dizziness.

Ken Brown was the first team centre-half in those days. He was another lively, friendly character, a good type to have around particularly when the team had lost. You never saw Ken in a bad mood. He was always smiling and happy. He followed John Bond to Gillingham and then Bournemouth when Bond went into management and for many years was the go-between between Bond and the players. When Bond left Norwich to take over as manager of Manchester City, he surprised a lot of people in the game by leaving Ken behind at Carrow Road and taking John Benson with him as his number two. Ken subsequently became the Norwich manager and still kept smiling and joking despite the pressures. I wonder whether he will be able to keep that up. To be successful in management sometimes you have to be a bit nasty and aggressive and that is alien to Ken's nature.

John Bond always spoke his mind as a player at West Ham. During team meetings, he would be the one to speak up and weigh in with a counter proposal. He always had this air of rebelliousness about him. He was his own man, an independent type with a droll sense of humour. On the field he could sometimes be undisciplined, racing off upfield at the wrong moments. Ron Greenwood always encourages his full-backs to attack but Bondy was often carried away by his enthusiasm.

The two other first team full-backs at the club in those days, Joe Kirkup and Jack Burkett, were much quieter characters. Joe, one of the nicest fellows in the game, later went to Southampton and then North America. Eddie Bovington, an under-rated performer, was the ball winner of the side in midfield, taking over the role from Andy Malcolm.

Filling the midfield dynamo role was Ron Boyce, whom the other players called 'Ticker' because he was like a watch – he never stopped. Ron was one of the unheralded heroes. He was rarely mentioned in the papers but the rest of the players appreciated what he did for the side. Amazingly, he used to smoke forty cigarettes a day and one wondered why he was not always coughing and spluttering. He still smokes today, probably heavier! Ron is the youth team coach at Upton Park and is still doing the club yeoman service.

John Sissons, the left winger, had the potential to become one of the best players West Ham have ever produced. Ron Greenwood always said he had the ability but somehow it was never quite realized. John was a very shy boy and if anyone had a go at him he would be like a hedgehog and disappear from view. This basic flaw in confidence can undermine the career of even the most talented of players. I had a similar problem myself but was helped over it by a number of good people. One person who was always reassuring me and building up my confidence was Jack Turner, the businessman and agent who was a friend of most of the West Ham players of that time. I will always be grateful to him for the part he played in seeing my career develop on and off the field.

Brian Dear vied with Sealey for the right to play up front alongside 'Budgie' Byrne and Geoff Hurst, and on occasions he was a prolific goalscorer. He once scored five goals against West Bromwich Albion. But he left the club after being involved in the Blackpool night club affair in 1971.

Jim Standen was the club's first choice goalkeeper in my early days at the club. He was a popular person and a steady goalkeeper whose catching was probably helped by being a first class cricketer with Worcestershire. He rarely made mistakes. In 1967 Ron Greenwood paid a world record fee of £65,000 for Kilmarnock goalkeeper Bobby Ferguson. We knew that

Ferguson would be arriving at the club but his transfer was delayed as Kilmarnock were in the Fairs Cup as it was known in those days and their manager was reluctant to release him until they were knocked out. Ron Greenwood also wanted to strengthen the centre-half position after Ken Brown's departure and he bought another Scot, John Cushley from Celtic for £30,000. Cushley was a very bright person and a hard, rugged player who unfortunately struggled in the air. This failing created problems for Bobby Ferguson; neither of them had a happy time in their first season and we had a spell when we were criticized for conceding too many soft goals.

Finding a partner for Bobby Moore in defence was one of the big problems and Alan Stephenson soon arrived from Crystal Palace for £80,000 to replace Cushley. Stephenson was much better in the air and had a good run in the side before a cartilage operation put him out of action, and another expensive centre-half arrived in Tommy Taylor, an £80,000 buy from Orient. When Stephenson was fit it created problems which Ron tried to solve by moving Tommy Taylor into midfield, unsuccessfully as it turned out.

I made my first team début in 1967 against Burnley at Turf Moor. The match ended in a 3-3 draw and I was fairly satisfied. Victor Railton, that loveable Cockney character who used to write most of the football for the London *Evening News* wrote at the time:

> West Ham may introduce 18-year-old Trevor Brooking to First Division football at Turf Moor tonight in their bid for the Double over Burnley.
> Despite a £130,000 outlay on three new defenders, Hammers have only one win from three games and may turn to local boy Brooking to liven their attack. Fast and powerful, Brooking is a current England Youth international with outstanding ability. He could link up with Geoff Hurst and prove as big a find as Everton's Joe Royle.

Vic, who had a close relationship with Ron Greenwood and Eddie Chapman – he went to school with Eddie – was well informed about the club's affairs throughout his long career in

Fleet Street but I think he may have slipped up with that description 'fast and powerful'. Some of my playing colleagues might disagree with him. When Vic used to ring up he always used strong language, not that anyone ever took offence. One day he rang me and my father took the call. 'Come on, you miserable old so and so,' said Vic. And he went on in similar vein until my father interrupted and asked who was calling. Vic thought he was talking to me. It made little difference. He was the same to everyone whether he knew them or not. Vic was also wrong when he said I would play in attack. I played in midfield on the right and did not try any heroics. First team football is invariably played at a much greater pace than reserve and youth football. Players not only move quicker but they think much quicker. It comes as quite a shock.

At the time, Burnley had a fair side which played a similar attacking style to our own. There were players of the calibre of John Angus, Ralph Coates, Martin Dobson, Gordon Harris, Willie Morgan, Andy Lochhead, Brian O'Neil and Dave Thomas in their side and eventually nearly all of them had to be sold to keep the club alive. With a population of less than 100,000 and with so many big city clubs round them, Burnley have had to perform miracles to survive in the highest company, only recently sinking to the second and then third Divisions.

Later that season, there were times when I played as a striker and I scored nine goals in twenty-three League matches but I knew I would never be another Geoff Hurst. I was not sharp enough to be a striker. I preferred to take defenders on face to face and not have to play with my back to goal.

I had two inconclusive years in and out of the side until Christmas 1969 when a defender clipped my ankle in a game against Nottingham Forest and I went off with what turned out to be a chipped bone. The forecast was that I would be out three weeks, but it was eight weeks, and by the time I was fit the club had signed another midfield player, Peter Eustace from Sheffield Wednesday, for £90,000. Eustace was a similar type of player to me and I could not see him, Martin Peters and myself all playing in the side. As the youngest of the three, I was the one to go out of the team.

That was a period of self doubt that nearly resulted in me

giving up the game. This fierce competition for places is very unsettling, but is inevitable in a fast-changing profession like professional football. In the City, company heads are not likely to rush out and buy a new executive whenever they feel the company needs strengthening. They might do it occasionally but not several times a year as happens in football. The uncertainty in the game creates a feeling that players have to make as much money out of it as they can before their turn comes to be replaced. That should be remembered when the critics start talking about greedy players.

Although this period of my career ended with worries, there had been happier moments, like the game against Newcastle in 1968 when I scored my one hat-trick. I still have the battered old ball in my study. It was also the time I became friendly with the present club captain Billy Bonds whose signing on 13 May 1967 for £50,000 from Charlton was in my view the club's most successful venture into the transfer market. We always share a room together on trips and get on exceptionally well. The only time there is any discord is at night over the time the light should go out. I usually want an extra minute or two to finish a chapter in a book while Bill will want to go to sleep. I never mind sharing a room. There is so much time to spare on trips that it would be lonely on your own. The club would not allow one person to a room anyway because of the cost. With England, I usually share with Kevin Keegan. We have a good understanding both on and off the pitch.

When Joe Kirkup left, West Ham experimented with Dennis Burnett, now coaching in Norway, at right-back before Bill was signed from Charlton. Bill started at right-back where he was an attacking defender in the West Ham tradition before Ron Greenwood switched him to midfield. He is such a good player with good, all-round skills that he can play anywhere in midfield or at the back. Scores of players inferior to him have been capped by England and I rate him one of the unluckiest players in the game not to have been selected for his country. The main reason he has been ignored is his unassuming, retiring personality. He is not a person who will willingly take the limelight. When a match is over, he will be one of the first players to be changed and on his way home. He is the complete family man, happiest when he is pottering around at his home at Sundridge Park. He is not much of a socializer. Some players are always being quoted in the newspapers and on television and if Bill had been like that I feel he would have gained a number of caps. He would have loved to play for his country.

When Ron Greenwood took over from Don Revie as England manager, he called Bill up for one of his squads but shortly afterwards he suffered a pelvic strain which affected him for nearly a year and the chance was lost. But the cruellest act was yet to come for at the end of the 1980-81 season Bill was selected for the England squad to play in the matches against Brazil and the Home Countries. Unbelievably, two days before joining the squad he broke a rib in a rearranged league fixture against Sheffield Wednesday and that coveted cap eluded him yet again. Nevertheless he remains the fittest player on the books at West Ham and I can see him playing for a few years to come. He is one of football's most inspirational figures and a credit to his profession.

4

In the Cold

The day I had to think seriously about whether I should continue in football came in 1971 when I was out of the side and earning only small bonuses in the reserves. It came home to me just how badly off we were when the window cleaner cleaned the windows of our semi-detached house in Clayhall and Hilkka had to hide in the bathroom because she did not have enough money to pay him! As it was she had to work for the first five years of our married life because we were so short of money.

I met Hilkka in 1968 at Tony's wedding to a Finnish girl, Ritva, when Hilkka was working as an au pair in Golders Green. It took me nearly three months to pluck up the courage to ring her and ask for a date and she certainly made me pay for my original hesitancy by saying she was 'too busy in the near future'. So it was almost three weeks later that we had our first date. I still chuckle when I think back to my efforts to make an early impression.

Having only just passed my driving test, it was a somewhat apprehensive individual who set out for London in a newly acquired Ford Anglia. My format for the evening was a visit to the cinema followed by dinner for two. Perhaps my selection of 'The Great Train Robbery' was not the most romantic but at least it was enjoyable. The candlelit dinner that followed materialized as coffee and a snack in the Golden Egg in Oxford Street. But despite this unglamorous beginning there was obviously something about me that she liked and within eight months we were engaged. We were married two years later, on 6 June 1970, when I was twenty-one.

Ron Greenwood has always advised players to marry young

as he did himself because it helps them mature and keeps them out of pubs and discos. My brother was best man and some of the players, including Billy Bonds, Bobby Howe, now in North America, and Harry Redknapp came as guests. Harry, who took over on the right wing from Peter Brabrook, was a terrific Cockney character. He had a spell in North America with Jimmy Gabriel at Seattle and now lives at Bournemouth. He helped Bobby Moore with the coaching at Oxford City.

I was dropped after the 1-4 home defeat by Derby County in 1971 and as the team won the next match 1-0 at Coventry, I knew it would be several weeks before I returned. Jimmy Lindsay, who was later sold to Watford, went out of the team at the same time. In fact, I was out for six months and it caused me many misgivings. I went to see Ron Greenwood and said perhaps a change of club would be best for me, but he said that as West Ham were in danger of being relegated – we finished in twentieth position – he was not going to release anyone from his contract. I went to see him again at the end of the season and I went on the transfer list. All that happens is that you become available for transfer and the manager notifies other clubs either by a circular letter or by personal contact. One or two journalists rang to say so and so club was supposed to be interested – Luton and Millwall were two clubs they mentioned – but I heard nothing officially. Even though they were not in the First Division I would have been willing to go to either club in order to gain regular first team experience. I do not think I could have continued much longer in reserve football.

Around this time I began to think more deeply about my game and how it was progressing, and I accepted Ron Greenwood's criticism that I should be more aggressive and more involved in matches. But I still could not stop harbouring doubts about whether I would ever make the grade. Playing in front of two or three hundred people in reserve matches is soul destroying and you reach the stage where you are secretly hoping that a first team player will break down, or lose form so that you can win your place back. That does not help team spirit.

Handling players who are in this position is one of the most

t the age of six with my
rother Tony, who was nine,
y mother Margaret and father
arry. I was the curly haired
ne in the family!

My second goal in England's 1981 World Cup qualifier victory over Hungary was the
inest shot I have ever struck. (*Photo*: Sporting Pictures)

Billy Bonds and I congratulate the hero of the 1975 Wembley Final, two-goal Alan Taylor. (*Photo*: The Press Association)

A distinguished gathering of TV men as I am presented with the 'Hammer of the Year' trophy for 1975-6. At the time Jimmy Hill, now presenter of 'Match of the Day', was working for ITV with Brian Moore of 'The Big Match'. Next to me is West Ham President Reg Pratt, and Ron Greenwood is on the left. (*Photo*: Tower Hamlet Studios)

rsuing Liam Brady at Wembley. I often have my tongue in my cheek when I'm aying! (*Photo*: Monte Fresco)

Some light-hearted badinage with former England manager Don Revie. Also takin part are Joe Corrigan (half hidden), Mike Doyle, Gordon Hill and the late Les Cocke (*Photo*: Monte Fresco)

Fame at last! A road is named after me in Forest Gate. The local council also named road after Bobby Moore. (*Photo*: Reg Lancaster)

difficult jobs a manager has to do. Man management is the most important of the many roles a manager has to perform. Some clubs such as Liverpool keep their first team squad happy by paying all of them the squad rate whether they are in the side or not, but many clubs cannot afford to do that. Rather than accept this 'non-person' role I think I would retire from the game and go into business. Many players drift from club to club in order to protect their status as full-time professionals but many of them would be better off taking a job outside the game and playing non-League football part time.

At the start of the 1971-72 season Tommy Taylor filled the number ten position with Alan Stephenson partnering Bobby Moore in defence. If Tommy had succeeded as a midfield player I might have left the club or even gone out of the game, but after the opening two matches which were defeats, 0-1 at home to West Bromwich Albion and 0-2 at Derby County, Greenwood moved him back to centre-half and dropped Stephenson. I was recalled in midfield and played there for the rest of the season. The crisis was over.

There were three other occasions when I might have left Upton Park. The first was during the 1972-73 season when Brian Clough offered West Ham £400,000 for Bobby Moore and me, equivalent to more than £1 million by today's standards. Judging from Clough's recent comments about my ability I think he really wanted Moore, not me. I must have been the lightweight in the transaction. The 'deal' was started when Clough met Nigel Clarke, the *Daily Mirror* soccer and tennis reporter, while watching the Wimbledon tennis championships. Clarke was writing a column for Bobby Moore in the *Mirror* at the time and when Clough said he would be interested in signing Bobby, he sensed a story. He called Bobby and told him about Clough's interest who gave him permission to pass on his ex-directory telephone number to Clough. Clough later rang Bobby and asked him to meet at Churchill's Hotel near Oxford Street, a property owned by the late Sir Eric Miller, the Fulham director who committed suicide. As they were about to go into the dining room for lunch the maître d'hôtel refused to let Moore in because he was casually dressed and did not have a tie.

Clough said: 'My team will never stay here again if my player cannot sit in this restaurant.' The maître d'hôtel relented and negotiations began over lunch. Derby already had two of the best central defenders in England in Roy McFarland and Colin Todd but Clough explained that he was intending to move Todd to full-back. After lunch, Clough tried to contact Greenwood and was told the West Ham manager was on holiday. The next Moore knew, the West Ham directors had agreed to accept in principle the £400,000 joint offer but Ron Greenwood refused to let us go. It was part of the West Ham way of doing things that the manager should have the final decision over letting players go. So we both stayed.

I cannot say I would have relished the idea of working for Brian Clough. I am not the kind of player who would take to public criticism too kindly. I am like Trevor Francis in personality and I know Trevor has not been too enraptured about some of the things Clough has said about him. Clough can be kind one minute, harsh and destructive the next. I am afraid I would take more notice of his strictures than his praise. Some players need this abrasive treatment and respond to it. I do not. Questioned by reporters once about the contribution of Stan Bowles in a match during Bowles's short stay at Nottingham Forest, Clough said: 'Bowles? Was he playing?' That may sound funny at the time, but it can be upsetting to the player concerned.

Despite the element of strain in his relationships with his players, Clough has the reputation of being an outstanding motivator. He earns his money in the time leading up to the kick off. Forest players have told me he is often not seen at the training ground in the week so it is not solely his coaching ability that has made Forest one of the most successful club sides in Europe in recent years. Clough's record of success has confirmed him as one of Europe's best managers. When Don Revie was in his final days as England manager there was a fair amount of public support for Clough to succeed him, but with the Football Association wanting stability after the dramas of Revie's last year, there was no chance of Clough taking over.

Ron Greenwood was just the man to provide the stability the FA wanted and it was a good idea to surround himself with some outstanding younger managers and coaches who could be groomed as possible successors. Clough was one of the management team and was given the England Youth team but his unpredictable nature soon caused friction and he resigned the post. It was used as a testing ground for him to provide evidence that he could conform, but he wasted the opportunity and I cannot see the FA giving him another job. He has admitted himself that he is out of the running. If Ron Greenwood retires after the 1982 World Cup the FA will want someone with his approach to carry on the reforms he started. They will be insisting on dignity as a prime requirement.

Clough has been accused of being defensive but I don't agree with that. His approach tends to be flexible, much more flexible for example than Revie's when he was at Leeds. With a full strength side, Clough will get his team to attack and on the occasions where he has been labelled defensive, as in the European Cup Final against Hamburg, the critics overlooked that he was without Trevor Francis. Garry Birtles was almost alone in attack. Tactically, what Clough did that night was a triumph because Hamburg looked to me to be the better side but still lost. Clough has also been criticized for defensive tactics when his side has played Liverpool, and it is true that he has pulled men back and tried to frustrate Liverpool. But here again he often came out on top against superior opposition so you cannot fault him. When he was at Derby County, he transformed them into an attractive attacking team which won the League championship.

The second occasion when there was a possibility of me leaving West Ham was in 1974 when there were rumours that Tottenham Hotspur had offered £425,000 for me. I was unsettled about pay and conditions at the time and once more the newspapers carried stories about my imminent departure. They seemed to know more about it than I did. Bobby Moore had just been allowed to join Fulham and with West Ham low in the First Division, there was speculation that several more players, me included, would be leaving. A move to Spurs would have been a great challenge. Bill Nicholson, their manager at the time, had a reputation for being one of the best buyers of talent in the game and had built one of the greatest club sides with his 1960s Double-winning team. By 1974, however, he was nearing the end of his distinguished reign at White Hart Lane and the pressure was building up round him.

The problem for a new player at Spurs was winning over a critical crowd. Several leading players, including Terry Venables and Alan Mullery, had had difficulty doing it. There was still an element in the crowd who compared every new signing with Dave Mackay and Danny Blanchflower. It was especially hard for a midfield player to be successful at the club. After he left Spurs to be succeeded briefly by Terry Neill, Bill Nicholson worked at West Ham as an assistant to Ron Greenwood and John Lyall. But it never worked out. Bill was too steeped in the White Hart Lane tradition and his heart was still at Tottenham. I remember after one game when we had drawn in the FA Cup he said: 'We'll beat them in the return at White Hart Lane!'

The rumour about me going to Spurs started while I was with England making my début in Lisbon, and on my return I went to see Ron Greenwood. We agreed to defer any action until the end of the season when we would see if the club had survived in the First Division. We just managed to stay up by finishing one point above Southampton who went down with 36 points.

The last and most difficult decision affecting my West Ham future came when we were relegated to the Second Division in May 1978. The prospect of a lower grade of football was not inviting and I was also concerned about how it would affect my England place with Ron Greenwood. However, Ron assured me that as long as he was happy with my form I would still be selected. In the end, with my family and business all in the area and the fact that the club and their supporters had always been so fair with me, I decided to choose contentment rather than ambition. Who was to know that in the following three years in the Second Division I would play in an FA Cup final and a League Cup final, get back into Europe and, of course, eventually gain that Second Division Championship medal? Some gifted players can go through their whole career without being fortunate enough to achieve even some of these honours. It was a very exciting period although without doubt the best part was getting back into the First Division.

In one of our talks, Ron Greenwood once asked me why I kept falling over during my matches. It happened so often that the other players called me 'Cyril' after the 'carpet King' Cyril Lord because I was always on the floor.

'It is a bad habit which you need to get out of your system,' he said. 'For someone of your height and weight you shouldn't be knocked off the ball so easily.'

The only explanation I could offer was that I had a long stride at the time and perhaps I was off balance more than I should have been. I worked on it in training and in recent years I feel I have conquered it. I do not go down so easily and I am more able to ride tackles from the side.

There are some players around these days who are always falling over, mainly inside the penalty area. Franny Lee was a master at it when he was at Manchester City and in one season he scored more than double figures in penalties. I cannot agree with the morality of 'diving' inside the box to trick a referee. Far better to try and go on and score if there is a chance. Often I see players go down when they might have put the ball in the net if they had shown more determination and less willingness to lay claim to an acting Oscar. Often feigning injury or taking a dive can react against a player. Since Mickey Thomas of Manchester United was seen winking on television after earning a penalty in a match I am sure referees have looked more sceptically at situations when he has been felled inside the box. There was an incident at Highbury towards the end of 1980 when he was brought down but he made such an exhibition of falling that the referee failed to give the penalty that even the Arsenal players had expected.

Although I had a reputation for falling down, I have only once been accused of diving. That was in the 1979-80 season during a Second Division match at Luton. Tony Grealish, Luton's Irish international, clipped my ankle as I was running into the box and I took a couple more strides before falling over. A penalty was awarded and David Pleat, the Luton manager, said afterwards that I had dived. I can quite honestly say that I had not tried to deceive the referee. I thought Grealish had been unlucky because I was running across him and his effort to knock the ball away was just enough to send me off balance. In fact, in fourteen years as a first team player, I have only had three penalties awarded for fouls against me, not a very high tally if I had been in the habit of diving. If I had been looking for penalties my total of goals would probably have quadrupled over the years and I would now be heading for the 200 mark. The reason why I am so seldom fouled in the danger area is that more often than not I am working wide of the box looking to play cross balls in. Or, if I am in the area, I am looking to score goals.

5

Moore, Hurst and Peters

It has always been said at Upton Park that West Ham won the World Cup for England in 1966. Geoff Hurst scored a hat-trick, Martin Peters scored the other goal and Bobby Moore was voted player of the tournament. It is certainly unique that one club should contribute so much and it reflected great credit on Ron Greenwood and everyone connected with West Ham.

I saw only one of the World Cup games in person, the semi-final against Portugal which England won 2-1. Eusebio and the other Portuguese players were gallant losers in that match, with the many Benfica players in their side equalling England in skill and endeavour. Eusebio was the player who made the headlines in that tournament, but the man who impressed me most was the captain, Mario Coluna, a stocky, strolling player who used the ball superbly. I suppose being slightly similar in style I appreciated greatly his skill. I also liked the Portuguese left-winger Antonio Simoes, a terrific little player who gave George Cohen a tough time. Bobby Charlton was the match winner, scoring both England goals. I sat in one of the cheap seats behind a goal and it was so instructive for an apprentice midfield player to see two such great and contrasting midfield players as Charlton and Coluna.

I watched the final against West Germany on television at home. It was one of the most dramatic World Cup finals of all time, but it would not have been had the Germans not equalized near the end. Extra time provided the nailbiting climax. Like everyone else, I was proud of England's performance and the part played by the West Ham trio.

Bobby Moore had the reputation with supporters of being

aloof from things, but he was not really. It was just that he found it difficult to mix and was not a great conversationalist, basically because he was on the shy side. He would never make the first approach at parties. He was a bit stiff and conscious of his position as captain and leader. He was never a person to relax and sit around. He was always getting up and going off somewhere and wanting to do things. All this helped make him something of a remote figure to younger players and most of them were slightly in awe of him. He was meticulously tidy. He would hang up his clothes in the right place and was always immaculately dressed and groomed. In his earlier days he shared a room with John Cushley at West Ham and in his later years had a room by himself which I think he preferred. You never felt you could get close to him. He was probably more friendly with 'Budgie' Byrne than with anyone else, but 'Budgie' was everyone's friend. He had his drinking friends from the club, including Byrne, Jimmy Greaves and Cushley and this tended to be a regular school.

His example taught me a lot early in my career because although he had outstanding ability he only became a great player by being very dedicated and determined to get to the top. He was very ambitious and worked extremely hard to perfect those parts of his game which were his hallmark. He would spend hours on the training ground dropping in balls from deep positions for the front players, and the West Ham fans saw the result on Saturday afternoons when he would find Geoff Hurst and 'Budgie' Byrne and turn defence into attack. Some players save their best work for the game but Bob never did. Everything had to be perfect down to the last five-yard ball in training. He was a domineering character on the pitch, always making himself available and wanting the ball. He did not say too much but his actions spoke louder than words. He was so dominating in fact that some of us tended to let him have the ball when it could have been better used elsewhere. Ron Greenwood was always telling us to accept more responsibility, but it was often difficult to assert oneself with Bobby Moore around. Ron gave Moore licence to make tactical changes in the first half of matches and the former would often say to us: 'You don't need me. Sort it out yourselves.'

But the fear of making a mistake could have been the breaking of me. I had seen young players being inhibited and failing to fulfil their potential. Fortunately it did not happen to me. Confidence at this stage of one's career is absolutely vital. One might have the ability, but if it is not developed a player is finished in professional football.

Leadership came naturally to Bobby Moore, and an example of his quick thinking and initiative came in a match in which I accidentally knocked out a referee. The referee was Eric Read of Bristol and he was running behind me when I suddenly changed direction and caught him with my elbow on the temple. He fell to the ground, obviously unconscious, and the game continued. It would have been interesting to know what would have happened if a foul had been committed or something had happened that needed a decision, but before anything like that could occur, Bob ran over to the stricken referee, seized the whistle and blew it to stop play.

Another occasion when he showed his leadership qualities was during our four-match League Cup semi-final against Stoke in 1972. West Ham won 2-1 at Stoke in the first leg and we mistakenly thought that should have been enough. But in the second leg a week later John Ritchie scored just before the end to make it 2-2 on aggregate. We were awarded a penalty two minutes from time and Gordon Banks made an amazing save from Geoff Hurst to give his side a replay. Geoff blasted it as he usually did and Banks went the right way to fist the ball over the bar. The third game at Hillsborough ended in a 0-0 draw and during the fourth game at Old Trafford Bobby Ferguson was injured in the first half and had to go off. Clyde Best, the big, black lad from Bermuda, was our stand-in goalkeeper, but when Moore held out the jersey to him he said: 'No way. Not tonight. I can't.' There were 49,247 spectators inside the ground and it was too much for him. No-one volunteered to go into goal, so without saying a word Moore put the jersey on himself. He even saved a penalty from Peter Dobing only for Dobing to score from the rebound. I managed to score one but it was not enough and we went down 2-3 on the night.

Stoke went on to beat Chelsea 2-1 in the final at Wembley, and I was pleased to see that George Eastham scored one of the goals. George was in his final season and it was fitting he should end with a medal. He was a genuine two-footed player with a superb touch and feel for the ball – half of his passes were struck with the outside of his foot. He was a much more skilled player than most of his rivals for an England shirt. Stoke had a hard pair of defenders in Alan Bloor and Dennis Smith but I always felt one of their key men was Mike Bernard, the ball-winner in midfield. With Dobing and Eastham attacking, Bernard used to fill in the gaps and did it so well that he was often the reason why Stoke won matches. His contribution was frequently overlooked. Up front, Terry Conroy looked a great player in the making, but he was unable to fulfil his potential.

The real trouble when you played Stoke, however, was Gordon Banks. I did not see him in action before 1966 so it is difficult to compare him with Peter Shilton and Ray Clemence. Overall I would say he was probably our best all-round goalkeeper. He did not make many mistakes and had no apparent weakness. Ray Clemence's strength is the way he comes off his line, timing his forays so brilliantly that he acts as a makeshift sweeper behind Liverpool's back four. Ray is also good at taking crosses whereas if Peter Shilton can be faulted, it is in this aspect of his play. Peter's reactions on the goal-line are fantastic, however, and it is worthwhile seeing him at work at an England training session. He will defy us to get the ball past him from the edge of the penalty area and the saves he makes are unbelievable. Not many goals are put past him.

Like me, Bobby Moore was a two-footed player although his right foot was the stronger. And just as I am, he was often criticized for lacking pace. He worked hard at improving his quickness off the mark and, added to his anticipation of events, that more than made up for his physical slowness. He was famous for the drag back tackle. If an opponent was running in the inside-right position somewhere near the right-hand touchline he would tackle with his right leg and, keeping his balance with his left hand on the ground, drag the ball back, turn and regain his feet to play the ball to safety. The average player in that situation would tackle with his left leg and knock the ball into touch. No one else perfected this tackle as he did. It said everything there was to say about Bobby Moore as a player.

The safety first way was not for him. He wanted to do it in style and use the ball creatively.

Occasionally the drag back tackle let him down and nowhere was this more dramatized than in the Chorzow Stadium, Katowice, on 6 June 1973. England needed a draw against Poland to improve their chances of qualifying for the World Cup Finals the following year. Early in the second half Moore called for a pass from Roy McFarland and as Lubanski, the Polish striker, closed down on him he elected to pull the ball across him with his right foot as he had done so often in his career. Lubanski just got a touch and the ball spun behind Moore. The momentum of Lubanski's run carried him into the path of the ball and he went on to beat Peter Shilton. It had not been Moore's day. The first goal, credited to Gadocha, had touched his boot before going in the net. That was virtually the end of a great international career. He played three more times for England to reach 108 caps, but when Poland came to Wembley in October for the return match Norman Hunter was given his role.

History repeated itself because just after half time Hunter found himself in almost the same position Moore had been in several months previously. Ninety-nine times out of a hundred Hunter would have belted the ball into touch, but he tried to pull it back Bobby Moore style and lost it. Gadocha was left out wide and quickly squared to Domarski who scored the goal that put England out of the Finals. Allan Clarke equalized with a penalty, but that remarkable goalkeeper Tomaszewski managed to hold out until the end. The Poles went on to have an excellent tournament in the 1974 World Cup, winning the runners-up match.

More than anything else, Bobby Moore will be remembered for his coolness. He always had time to do what he wanted to do, with very few exceptions, and he sometimes broke the rules to do it. Frequently he would dribble the ball out of defence before delivering a pass and his control was so good that he was rarely dispossessed. I cannot remember seeing him lose his temper. In the many inquests we had in the West Ham dressing room, I never once heard him shout anyone down. He was a dignified figure both on and off the pitch.

Despite his worldwide reputation, he was not able to get a managerial job with a League club when he retired as some people had been expecting. I was not surprised. Of the three West Ham World Cup stars, I thought he was the least likely to step straight into management because of his reserved personality. One of the most vital aspects of management is understanding and mixing with people and that was never Bobby's strongest point. In terms of respect, Bobby led the field – his record was impeccable and his ability as a player unquestionable. Nobody could possibly say to him 'How many caps did you get?' in an attempt to belittle him.

But there is more to management than respect as Billy Wright and Bobby Charlton, similar personalities, discovered when they went into it. Both were too straight and too honest to handle all the problems that arose and they are now successful in other fields. Bobby Moore had a spell as part-time manager of the Berger Isthmian League side Oxford City and he spends most of his time helping to run five pubs successfully with Jimmy and Patsy Quill.

Geoff Hurst, who was Chelsea's manager until summer 1981, always looked to have managerial talent. He had a confident, bubbly personality and was a good mixer. And underneath it all was a slightly ruthless, determined streak which is needed to run a football club. I always thought he had the qualifications to perform the two basic tasks of the manager, to put his ideas over and to strike up a friendly but respectful relationship with his players. Despite Geoff's setback at Stamford Bridge, I am sure he has learnt a great deal and that other opportunities will arise. John Lyall, too, has both these assets.

Geoff Hurst started his footballing career as a strong, hard-working midfield player, but Ron Greenwood moved him to centre-forward and it must rank as one of the most successful positional changes in the history of English football. Geoff's greatest skill, which he worked at tremendously hard, was his ability to control and shield the ball from his marker so he could lay it off or turn and shoot. He had one of the fiercest shots in the game. Not for him the precise placement of a Jimmy Greaves. He was a two-footed finisher with equal power in both feet and the ball either ballooned the back of the net or finished up on the terraces. He used to puff out his cheeks as he struck the ball and there must be hundreds of pictures of him doing this. Most players have some odd quirk about them. Mine is to push my tongue into the side of my cheek, usually the right, as I run on the ball. I do not know I am doing it, I am concentrating so hard.

West Ham did not invent the near-post header but we developed it into a fine art and Geoff Hurst's goal against Argentina in the 1966 World Cup was one of the finest examples. Opposing sides were so wary of it that often we had to forsake it and attack the far post instead. There was no better exponent of the near-post header than Geoff Hurst.

Martin Peters was always the last mentioned when West Ham's World Cup trio were discussed, and a quiz question which does not always produce the correct answer when put to most soccer fans is: 'Who scored England's other goal in the 1966 World Cup?' Martin, ghostlike and stealthy on the field, tended to be ignored off it and I am sure that was one of the reasons why he eventually left West Ham in 1970. He was the first of the three to go. Martin is a calm, unemotional man, reserved in company, but has a wry sense of humour and enjoys a laugh. His somewhat pointed nose has earned him a fair amount of ribbing over the years. Born near Upton Park at Plaistow, he came up through the club's youth system and made his début in 1962. Two years later when West Ham reached the FA Cup Final, he experienced his first major disappointment when he was left out of the Final side and Eddie Bovington, a much different type of player, took his place.

One asset which made him a regular first team player after that, in addition to his undoubted ability, was his capacity to play in a variety of positions. If there was a hole to fill, he would fill it. He played most of his England games on the left side in midfield, but was chiefly a right-footed player and was more suited to the right side. Tall and slim, he looked ungainly at times when he ran. However, his running was hardly noticed because he nearly always arrived in a position at the same time as the ball. He was essentially a one touch player and he saw openings very early. He would play balls into gaps which opponents thought were not there. It was probably this perceptive quality which led Sir Alf Ramsey to say that he was ten years ahead of his time, one of the most quoted remarks of recent times. Players get labels attached to them and that was Martin's and it undoubtedly put pressure on him. I do not think Alf genuinely thought that Martin was a 1976 player when he said it but it was his way of drawing attention to a thoughtful player who was not getting the recognition he deserved. Martin scored some magnificent goals for West Ham and the one I remember most was a fantastic volley from a John Sissons cross very similar to the one Graeme Souness scored in one of the television 'Goal of the Season' competitions.

I think Martin lasted as a player longer than Moore and Hurst because he was a midfield player and experience can get you by more in midfield than at the back or in attack. When a defender starts to lose his pace he can be exposed and similarly a front player can be caught out more easily when he begins to slow down. Geoff Hurst's retirement was hastened by a back injury which never properly cleared up. Being knocked in the back by the defenders so often could not have helped it. In midfield, the play goes on round you and your mistakes are not highlighted as much as say a defender's missed tackle or a front player's miss-hit shot in front of an open goal. This is why some of the longest-serving players, such as Alan Ball, John Hollins, John McGovern, Archie Gemmill and myself, operate in midfield.

When Martin left West Ham in March 1970, the fee of £200,000, which included a valuation of £54,000 for Jimmy Greaves, was a British transfer record. Tottenham gained an international midfield player who was still in his prime whereas West Ham obtained the services of a once-great player who no longer had a zest for the game. We all loved Jimmy Greaves. He had a lovely way about him, warm and friendly, but as a player he never got started with us. He scored twice on his début against Manchester City at Maine Road but only managed thirteen goals for West Ham in just under two seasons. For a time, Ron Greenwood had him playing in midfield. Jimmy was disillusioned about how the game was going. He thought defenders were getting too much licence to kick the good players, and the tighter disciplinary measures introduced by the Football League in 1971 came too late to keep him in the game.

He had already decided to retire and go full-time into his three businesses. I always remember him saying at a social evening: 'If people are asked who I played my best football for, Chelsea supporters will say Chelsea, Spurs supporters will say Spurs and West Ham supporters will say either Chelsea or Spurs.' He was thirty-one when he retired prematurely, a considerable loss to the game because no player of his ability has emerged since then.

Martin Peters' move to Tottenham helped advance my career at Upton Park because we were similar in styles. However, it took a couple of years before I capitalized on his departure. At White Hart Lane, Martin was given the captaincy and went on to enhance his already considerable reputation. No longer was he in the shadow of Bobby Moore and Geoff Hurst. He took part in many memorable triumphs at Spurs before moving on to Norwich. Joining John Bond at Carrow Road was a good move for him because Bond was also a West Ham man and knew how to get the best out of him. Their footballing philosophies were similar. Martin was able to play First Division football well into his mid-thirties and it was not a case of him being carried by other players. He continued to score goals at the same rate as he had scored them at West Ham and Spurs, one every three-and-a-half matches, and was an inspiring captain. With their limited time at top level, Norwich needed someone of his vast experience. I thought he would finish his playing days there and join the coaching staff, but to everyone's surprise, he joined Third Division Sheffield United as player-coach before becoming team manager, only to quit after the 1980-81 season.

Not many southern players settle successfully in the North and I found Martin's move perplexing. I would certainly be extremely reluctant to join a northern club when all my connections, as Martin's are, lie in the London area. Also, emphasising the difficulties in switching from one role to another, Sheffield United were relegated to the Fourth Division when Walsall converted a penalty against them with five minutes remaining in their last League fixture. To worsen the agony Sheffield were awarded a penalty themselves two minutes later – and missed!

6

The Family Club

No club in the Football League has such an affinity with its fans as West Ham. It is truly a family club, and the 24,000 fans who regularly attend matches at Upton Park are part of that family. This spirit derives from a variety of factors, from the club's location in the East End of London, from its people and from its history. Above all it is based on the wit of the East Ender. The underlying feeling at Upton Park is a contented one, both within the club and on the terraces and in the stands. You will hear more wisecracks at Upton Park than at most grounds. You are also likely to hear much more encouragement and much less abuse. When West Ham went behind in a match – and there were many times in the past few years when that happened – the reaction of the crowd was to try to lift the home players. If a West Ham player won the ball and passed it to a colleague they would cheer. When the move broke down and an opponent gained possession, they booed. That sounds an almost childish way of behaving, but it has to be remembered that thousands of people in the crowd are school children anyway. Such reactions are still vented today and the players like it. In terms of loyalty, there is no better crowd anywhere, and that includes Liverpool supporters.

It was significant in the 1980-81 season that while attendances fell all over the country, even at Anfield, the gates at Upton Park rose by twenty per cent. In the previous season only Chelsea with 488,581 and Newcastle with 490,252 bettered West Ham's total of home fans, 480,321, and away from home West Ham were the most popular side in the Division with 388,470 spectators watching their games.

At each home game a mascot leads the team out and is usually given an encouraging reception. There is one who stands out in my memory, a fair haired boy of six who was the mascot for the FA Cup tie against Wrexham on 3 January, 1981. The 30,000 crowd (an amazing attendance in view of the opposition) really took to him and roared encouragement as he dribbled up to Phil Parkes and 'scored' from close range. During the match Frank Lampard was injured and needed treatment. While Rob Jenkins, the physiotherapist, was swabbing down his nose, they chanted: 'Bring on the mascot!'

The club is known as the 'Hammers', but the fans know it as 'The Irons' because it started life in 1895 as the Thames Iron Works Football Club. The players were recruited from a shipbuilding yard on the banks of the River Thames and the club was reorganized into West Ham United Football Club in July 1900. Descendants of the iron workers who founded the original club are still active with the present-day club. The president, Reg Pratt, has been connected with the club for nearly seventy years, as a youthful supporter, son of a director and from 1950 to 1979 chairman. The present chairman, Len Cearns, is the son of a former chairman and serves with his brother, Will Cearns, the club's solicitor director and Brian Cearns FCIS, another brother. Len's son, Martin Cearns AIB, is also a director. For one family to dominate a board of directors in such a way for so many years is remarkable and the position the club now enjoys is testimony to the sound way they have run the club's affairs. The only person outside the Cearns family on the board is the club's financial director Jack Petchey who joined in 1978 in succession to the late Mr Brandon. The board's philosophy is to let the professionals get on with the job, and it is a successful one. You do not see Len Cearns quoted in the newspapers about what he intends to do at West Ham. If it is a matter affecting the playing staff, John Lyall will be the policymaker. Administrative decisions are taken by Eddie Chapman, the chief executive. Eddie, who still plays cricket, joined West Ham's office staff in 1937 and was secretary for twenty-four years before he took up his present post.

The directors do not treat the players in an employer-employee manner. They regard them as friends. Every year they stage a party for the players and their wives and also a party for their children. And at Christmas each player is presented with a turkey.

The affinity with the East End is helped by the fact that most of the players were born near the ground – Billy Bonds, Paul Allen, Paul Brush, Pat Holland, Geoff Pike, Nicky Morgan, Glen Burvill, Frank Lampard, Everard La Ronde, Keith McPherson, Jimmy Neighbour, Wayne Reader, Mark Smith, Robert Wall and myself are all from within a few miles of Upton Park. In the past, almost all the staff came from the East End. Of the 1964 FA Cup final side, only Jim Standen and Johnny Byrne were not locals. In recent years this has changed as other clubs have started recruiting players from East London. Jerry Murphy, now with Crystal Palace, was an example of a fine young player who was signed from our area. At the same time the standard of schoolboy football has dropped in the area so West Ham have been forced to buy expensive players from other parts of the country.

In the early 1970s, Crystal Palace made a point of recruiting most of the best young players in London. Some clubs pay inducements to the fathers of promising players to make sure they sign for them, but West Ham have never done this. In recent years we have regained the monopoly of young talent in the area principally by stepping up our scouting efforts and also by offering higher wages.

Liverpool have been Britain's greatest team since 1945. This is based on a stable set-up at the club which makes sudden changes unnecessary. West Ham is another club which has tried to be just as stable. In managerial terms, West Ham have made fewer changes than Liverpool. There have only been five managers in the club's eighty-one-year history – Syd King, who was succeeded in 1931 by Charlie Paynter, Ted Fenton (1950-61), Ron Greenwood (1961-74) and John Lyall (1974-). All but Ron were players with West Ham. No other League club, not even Liverpool, can compete with this record. Liverpool have had only five managers since 1945 – George Kay, Don Welsh, Phil Taylor, Bill Shankly and Bob Paisley – but many more before it. Most of West Ham's backroom staff are locals too, including chief scout Eddie Baily, youth coach Ron Boyce, Tony Carr, another youth coach, reserve physiotherapist Dave Gladstone, Ernie Gregory and first team physiotherapist Rob Jenkins. The remaining coach on the staff, Mick McGiven, born in Newcastle, was formerly a West Ham player.

The three clubs which have the best records for not making changes are Liverpool, West Ham and Ipswich, and it is no coincidence that they have all had their share of trophies in recent years. Not many clubs are strong enough to be able to follow their example. As a club goes through a bad patch, fans start agitating and the directors are pressurized into sacking the manager and appointing someone else. The manager and those who have worked closely with him go and a new team with new ideas moves in. If the new man is unsuccessful and does not produce a winning team, he goes too and the process is repeated. Gerry Francis, the former England captain, claims he has played under sixteen club managers in his career – more than one a year. I have played under two, Ron Greenwood and John Lyall, both men of similar ideas about how the game should be played. I think I can count myself lucky.

There have been times when sections of the Upton Park crowd have become unsettled, particularly when we have been fighting relegation. The threat of dropping into the Second Division was with us for several seasons in the 1970s and after some close calls, we went down in 1978. All through this difficult period the bulk of the fans remained loyal. No fan wants to see his or her team go down but I had the impression that if we did, the supporters would still turn up. That was precisely what happened. If I met fans in the street or in shops or restaurants, they would pass on advice. There was little criticism and no hostility. Of course, no crowd is perfect and there have been occasions when our fans have barracked players. Mervyn Day was an outstanding example of a player whose confidence was affected by the jibes of spectators. That was the one time in my years at Upton Park that the supporters have upset a player. However, Merv has regained his confidence at Orient and is now a fine goalkeeper again.

Some clubs are always involved in controversy but little happens at West Ham to cause headlines, other than the way the team is playing. The Blackpool affair in 1971 was the exception when Bobby Moore, Brian Dear, Jimmy Greaves and Clyde Best were disciplined for drinking the night before a match. The incident only became generally known because a supporter rang the newspapers. The West Ham way is to deal with any breach of discipline internally and not to make it public. Ron Greenwood, and John Lyall, both believe in moderating their public statements to serve the best interests of the teams they manage. This is why both of them do not face the press until about twenty minutes after matches. Sometimes there are moments in a game, an offside that is not given, for example, which results in a point being lost, that can upset both players and managers. If the manager emerges within minutes of the final whistle to give interviews, he might say something he may later regret. Greenwood and Lyall try not to put themselves in that position.

I think the press and radio have an important role to play in promoting football, and interviews are a vital part of that promotion. Publicity about players sustains interest and stimulates people to go to matches. Years ago football reporters would write a blow-by-blow account of matches and that satisfied their readers. But today there is a wider demand for information. The public usually knows the scores and League positions early on Saturday evenings and the late-night TV soccer programme gives them all the action. The Sunday newspaper reports now have to go beyond merely reporting who scored the goals and how they were scored. There are also the Monday morning papers whose writers will be looking for a fresh angle. So the more interviews the reporters obtain the more chance they have of writing something fresh and interesting.

I agree there are occasions when a bad image can be put over if an unwise comment is given too much publicity but on the whole I think the British press does the game of football a great service. I do not believe there is too much exposure or too many interviews.

English football has some way to go before it matches what goes on in American sports. There reporters have the right to go into dressing rooms at a stipulated time after matches in the

North American Soccer League and can interview whoever they like. The League officials see this as an important way of promoting the game and a similar 'open door' policy predominates in most sports in America.

John Lyall let the press in immediately after West Ham's League Cup semi-final victory over Coventry in February 1981, and it worked well although the dressing room was rather packed! I could not remember this happening before at the club. But what happens when the press enter the losing team's dressing room? As was shown in the Granada TV documentary about Manchester City, beaten players usually sit dejectedly after matches and say nothing and I imagine it would be very hard to interview someone in that situation! The open door policy might eventually come in this country but first our younger players will have to be advised about how to handle the press.

Most clubs here, including West Ham, take the line that there must be some privacy. The fans do not have to know absolutely everything that is happening at a club. West Ham have always had a good image within the game and the right thing is usually said at the right time.

However, it is impossible to prevent every moment of discord and anger from being reported in the press. One such incident that was leaked was the punch up between Billy Bonds and Ted MacDougall in the shower after a 4-1 defeat at Leeds. A mix-up between them had led to one of the goals and the row continued in the dressing room, breaking one of the club's unwritten laws that flare ups on the pitch should not lead to bitter recriminations afterwards. It did not need much to rub Ted up the wrong way. He could be very acidic in his comments and this particular row led to blows being exchanged, and the two players had to be pulled apart. I was outside in the dressing room at the time and did not see what actually happened. Ted was not at the club for long after that. He was an excellent goalscorer but his limitations in the build-up play caused him to be frustrated. He was a short fuse character whose language and manner were inclined to upset some people.

Swearing, whether one accepts it or not, is part of the game. Kevin Keegan has written that I never swear and when I do I say

something like 'Oh scum'. This is not quite true. I do have a
quiet curse at myself sometimes when I make a mistake. But I
do not condone swearing at opponents or the referee, or at one's
colleagues. A player's confidence is not helped if someone is
cursing him in public.

Each person on a football field is different in temperament.
My temperament is equable and easy going, but I appreciate
that there are other players who are more excitable and liable to
get into trouble and I do not condemn them for it. Bill Bonds is a
good example. In his early days at the club he sometimes let
himself be involved in incidents, particularly with referees, yet
off the field you could not meet a quieter, more placid
individual. For Ron Greenwood or John Lyall to have
attempted to change him too much would have harmed his
value to the side. Without that one hundred per cent
commitment and aggression, he would not have been the same
player. In recent years, Bill has learned to count to ten before
reacting and it has paid off. We were very glad that he was the
one to stay after the Leeds incident. Nobody is more respected
at the club.

On the field, more swearing is done through frustration than
anything else. When a team is playing well and winning, you do
not hear much of it. Most referees will let it go, but there are
some who will stop the game and make a point of lecturing the
offender. For a player to use this type of language directly at the
referee is asking for trouble. It is like being rude to a traffic
policeman and can be just as expensive.

West Ham supporters come from all over the south-east of
England. Our catchment area extends to Hertfordshire in the
north-west and to Southend in the east. And some idea of their
loyalty to the players can be gauged from the size of the crowds
that attend testimonial matches at Upton Park. The crowd for
my match against an England XI drew a record 23,000 and
receipts were £25,000 after expenses had been met. Billy Bonds'
testimonial drew 21,000 fans in 1978 and Frank Lampard's
16,000. At most clubs attendances for testimonials have fallen
away so badly that some are thinking of discontinuing them
altogether. West Ham is the exception.

7

Cup Triumphs

On the Wednesday before the 1980 FA Cup final, Peter Watson, a journalist friend of mine, called my home to tell me that the sports editor of the *Daily Express*, Ken Lawrence, had asked him to warn me that Brian Clough had written a critical piece about me. 'The article is a bit unkind and Ken didn't want you to think the paper was being disloyal to you,' he said.

Peter had written four articles with me in the *Daily Express* about the Cup final against Arsenal and they were finishing Cup week with Clough's summing-up on the Saturday morning. 'What's Cloughie said?' I asked. Peter read it over. The headline was 'Now a stinging view of butterfly Brooking' and the story read:

Trevor Brooking floats like a butterfly . . . and stings like one. I have never had a high opinion of him as a player. He has been lucky enough to become a member of teams that he shouldn't really have had a sniff at.

I believe his lack of application and that of other players like him have meant relegation for West Ham in the past and the failure to win promotion this time. Wembley is made for a player like Alan Devonshire. He is young, in form and full of enthusiasm.

Brooking will only be able to have an influence on this Cup final when Devonshire or another of his willing team mates has battled to win it at the front or at the back so that he can pick it up in midfield.

Clough went on to complain about the lenient treatment Billy

Bonds had received from an FA Disciplinary Commission that had enabled him to play at Wembley, while another Commission had earlier stopped Larry Lloyd, a Nottingham Forest player, from appearing in the League Cup Final. That might have been the real reason for his attack not just on me, but on West Ham. His article ended with an indictment of us for allegedly ducking out of the promotion race to make sure we won a cup.

'It baffles me to hear some of their players bleat on about preferring promotion,' he said. 'They should have thought about that in January. If they had channelled as much energy into getting out of the Second Division as they have into reaching Wembley, they would have done it.'

By that time, of course, West Ham were out of the promotion race. From being fifth on 1 March we dropped to eighth by the end of March with four defeats in five matches. It was just something that occurred in the midst of the usual pile up of fixtures that happens when a club is chasing two prizes. There was certainly no intention to put winning the FA Cup before promotion.

Clough's attack provided some material for the television interviewers to follow up during the pre-match programmes on the morning of the final, but I would not be drawn into having a dig back at him. I did not want Cloughie to be able to claim afterwards that he had motivated me, especially as I had scored the only goal. I have to admit that when Peter Watson read the article over to me I was a little hurt, but by the time Saturday came round I had put it to the back of my mind. If Clough wanted to try and inject some controversy into the pre-match buildup that was up to him. Perhaps that was what upset him – he does not like my equable temperament and was trying to rile me!

The timing of his remarks was a little unsettling because it was the big talking-point during the hours before the match. I wondered what people would have said if I had had a poor game. They would have said: 'Brian Clough could be right.' It could have affected my England career – and it would have been grossly unfair for millions of people to have judged me on one game.

However, instant reactions and comments have become a part of football. A player is judged on his last game with little regard for previous matches. That is why I think television panellists on football programmes, and others who are hired to express views, should sometimes be more careful before they come to a judgment about a player. Lawrie McMenemy, one of the BBC panellists, asked me on 'Match of the Day' whether Clough's attack had geed me up and I said it had not because, fortunately, I knew about it three days earlier. Criticism like that might have upset a younger player but having played more than 500 games I could take it.

Before the replay of the 1981 FA Cup final between Spurs and Manchester City Clough once again upset one of the finalists on the morning of the match. This time he announced that he would like to buy Glenn Hoddle whose contract was coming to an end. I doubt whether he would have appreciated such timing if he had been in Keith Burkinshaw's shoes, coming as it did just at the moment when a manager wants the players' thoughts solely concentrated on the forthcoming match, not on speculation about transfers.

I do not know why Clough dislikes me so much, except that we are opposites and that might have provoked him. I have only met him once, at a function at the Sportsman Club in London early in my career. After the 1980 Cup Final he continued to attack me during the 'Michael Parkinson Show'. I did not see the programme myself but my parents told me about it. Warren Mitchell, the actor who plays West Ham fan Alf Garnett, was appearing on the same programme and he defended me. If Clough thought I was such a bad player I wondered why he tried to buy me once.

Although I scored the winning goal, the 1980 final will probably be remembered as Paul Allen's final. At 17 years and 256 days old, Paul (known as 'Ollie' at Upton Park after the Stan Oliver of Laurel and Hardy fame) was the youngest-ever Wembley finalist, taking the record from Howard Kendall who had played for Preston against West Ham in 1964. Paul, a very likeable youngster who looks younger than his years, ran tirelessly and shackled Liam Brady so effectively that Brady was unable to repeat the damage he inflicted on Manchester

United in the 1979 Final, when he played a part in all three
Arsenal goals. Paul did not tight mark him Italian style, but
whenever Brady had the ball he hustled and harried him and
Brady does not like that. He likes to be given time to get the ball
on his left foot and look up to see where he can deliver it with a
twenty- or thirty-yard pass. The climax of Paul's great day was
nearly scoring a goal two minutes from time, when with only
Pat Jennings to beat, he was tripped from behind by Willie
Young. He won the hearts of millions of people who were
watching round the world by getting up and shaking Willie's
hand.

Inside football the professional foul, as it is called, is accepted
as part of the game and it will remain so as long as the
punishment meted out is only a ticking off or a caution. Willie
was shown the yellow card by referee George Courtney and
acknowledged it like a man who knows he shouldn't have
parked on a double yellow line and politely thanks the traffic
warden for his ticket. When the ninety-two League chairmen
met the following season they said they wanted the professional
foul to be a sending off offence and I agree with that.
Deliberately pulling a player down when he is about to score
should warrant a sending off. While it ranks as only a
cautionable offence, defenders will continue to do it. Willie's
'tackle' received such widespread publicity that it probably
hardened the views of a lot of influential people in the game
trying to eradicate such play. I expect most players would have
done exactly as Willie did in the same circumstances. That is the
way professionals behave on the field. You are expected to do it.
But if players were sent off, attitudes would soon change.

Before the final, we did not think Arsenal's four games
against Liverpool before they qualified to meet us with a 1-0 win
in the third replay at Coventry had been too weakening on their
stamina. They still seemed to be full of running. But we
discovered at Wembley that two of their key players had been
shattered by it, strikers Frank Stapleton and Alan Sunderland.
They played like tired men. I had thought for some time that
the basis of Arsenal's success rested on the selfless running of
these two. Arsenal's system meant they were always
outnumbered two to one when the ball was played up to them

and they had to be good enough to hold the ball until reinforcements arrived from midfield. Up to the final they had kept doing this. Now they had little energy left and their tiredness also counted against Arsenal the following Wednesday in Brussels when they played Valencia in the final of the European Cup Winners' Cup. After drawing 0-0 at the end of extra time, Arsenal lost 4-5 on penalties. In five days, two major prizes had been snatched from them.

Our success against Arsenal at Wembley was a tactical success for John Lyall. When he and Eddie Baily watched them in three of their four matches against Liverpool they agreed that David O'Leary and Willie Young were the strength of the defence. The quartet who were the life force of the team were O'Leary and Young at the back and Stapleton and Sunderland at the front. John decided that West Ham's best chance of a narrow victory – no side, not even Liverpool, was ever going to score three or four goals against Arsenal on a neutral ground – was to take a front player out of the attack leaving O'Leary with no one to mark. The player John picked for the role was Stuart Pearson, who had been out injured for two weeks. Stuart was played in midfield in a free role and gave us a spare man to use when we were in trouble. After half an hour O'Leary was shouting to the bench: 'I've got no one to mark.' We expected Don Howe and Terry Neill to make adjustments at half time, but in the second half Arsenal were still content to let David Cross take on their whole back four. O'Leary should have gone into midfield much earlier and the full-backs should also have pushed up. With Graham Rix and Brady also playing deep roles, we were able to contain Arsenal in safe areas for much of the game. The neutral view was that it had not been a classic game and that was a fair assessment. Except for a Rix shot, a shot straight at him from Brian Talbot and another from Brady into the side netting, Phil Parkes had one of his quietest games.

We all felt sorry for Crossey. He had been sacrificed in the team plan and had done a tremendous amount of running without much reward or glory. When I scored the goal he said wryly: 'You lucky bastard.' I think he would have liked to put one in. For his efforts he had earned our respect and admiration. In the coach afterwards he came in and shouted: 'Anyone seen my legs? I've run them off and can't find them.'

He is one of the wittiest personalities in the game and a brilliant mimic. Once at Swansea, Bill Bonds wanted to use the toilet, but the door was locked. 'Who's in there?' he shouted. 'Come on, I can't wait.' A squeaky piping voice replied: 'Sorry Bill, it's me. Won't be long.' Bill thought it was Paul Allen but out stepped Crossey. He can mimic most of the players and is one of the club's top performers in quizzes. He has a lot of 'O' and 'A' levels and is one of the most intelligent footballers in the game. His favourite relaxation is reading, and he reads some hefty works. The crowd know him as 'Psycho' because there have been one or two occasions when he has lost his temper and has been involved in incidents with an opponent. But to the players he is Norman. One day at training Ernie Gregory shouted at him 'Come on, Norman', and the name stuck. Ernie could not believe he had said it. There was not a Norman on the staff and no one could ever remember one.

David is as good a volleyer or half-volleyer of a ball as I have ever seen. He is slight in build for a striker and that makes him much more mobile than the average goal-scorer. He has turned out to be one of John Lyall's best buys. It is a coincidence that the key strikers in our two successful FA Cup campaigns should both have begun their careers at Fourth Division Rochdale. Alan Taylor, like Cross, started at Spotland. Crossey remains their most expensive export. He brought in £40,000 plus a player, Malcolm Darling, when Norwich bought him in 1971.

As I left home on Friday before the Cup Final, Collette, my daughter, asked: 'Are you going to score a goal for me, Daddy?' I said I would try, but I was not too confident. This was a view shared by the bookmakers who quoted long odds of 16-1 for me to score the first goal. Consequently the goal in the thirteenth minute was something of a surprise. Alan Devonshire set off on a run down the left and his acceleration left Talbot and Pat Rice behind as he reached the by-line and crossed. Pat Jennings just got a touch and the ball flew to Cross on the right of the box. Dave's shot was blocked by Young and came out to Pearson who was at a fairly tight angle on the right. Stuart instinctively tried a shot, scooping the ball across the box instead of at goal and I realized I had only to reach it with my head to score. I fell backwards and managed to steer the ball goalwards. I knew it was a score as soon as I connected. I had a quick look at the referee to see there was no offence and hared off towards the left-hand touchline with arms raised. I do not know why I went in that direction: there were few West Ham fans in that part of the stadium. Bill Bonds grabbed me demanding: 'What are you doing scoring with your head?' It was only the third or fourth time I had ever headed a goal.

I was so elated in the dressing room afterwards that I had a sip of champagne – usually I am teetotal. And I also had a glass of champagne during a late night dinner at the Inn on the Park afterwards. I left the club's banquet at the Grosvenor House Hotel quite early to meet some friends for a meal. While we were eating, a waiter brought a bottle of champagne indicating that it was with the compliments of some people sitting nearby. I looked across at the friendly faces. 'When you've finished that one, there's another here for you,' said a man. 'We're from the north-east and my team Sunderland is playing your lot on Monday.' He thought a heavy night's drinking might help Sunderland beat us and gain promotion. I did not let on that I was a teetotaller. The friends on my table enjoyed the wine. If West Ham had won at Roker Park, Chelsea, not Sunderland, would have gone up. There were 45,000 fans there and we lost 0-2. And afterwards I had some more champagne with Bryan Robson as we celebrated our successes.

The bookmakers made us outsiders all the way through the 1980 Cup campaign and that helped us. We were second favourites from the third round when we drew 1-1 with West Bromwich Albion at the Hawthorns. Only Frank Lampard, Pat Holland, Bill Bonds and myself survived from the 1975 FA Cup-winning side which showed what a vast number of changes take place in even the most stable of football clubs. Mervyn Day, Keith Robson, Alan Taylor, Bill Jennings, Kevin Lock, John McDowell and Graham Paddon had all gone. It was virtually a new team. Two youngsters with a brilliant future ahead of them were now stalwarts in defence alongside Bill Bonds and Frank Lampard – Scots utility defender Ray Stewart and Bootle-born Alvin Martin at centre-half. We discovered when we played Dundee United in a friendly that Ray was known as 'Tonker'. It is a nickname that has stuck with him at Upton Park. When he gets the ball, he tends to drive it. Defensively, there are not many young defenders who are better in the Football League, but we are working on the distribution side of his game. Alvin Martin has the reputation of being a strong, determined player yet he is also very skilful. He had so much skill when he was younger that he had a tendency to dribble out of the box and occasionally give away a needless goal. Since Billy Bonds has played alongside him, he has overcome this weakness and in May 1981 he gained his first England cap against Brazil. We call him 'Stretch' because he is a leggy player who seems to be able to stick a leg or a toe out to knock the ball away. In addition to the new defenders, we also had two new strikers in Stuart Pearson, one of the unluckiest players with injuries in my time in football, and David Cross in place of Robson, Jennings and Taylor.

'Pop' Robson had come and gone. 'Pop' left the club in 1974 and we went on to win the FA Cup, and the same thing happened after he left us for the second time in 1979. He thought he had a business opportunity in the north-east so he signed for Sunderland. Unfortunately the venture never materialized. I think he wished he had stayed at Upton Park. He was one of the most popular players on the staff. I have never seen a better finisher than Robson. He could turn and shoot with both feet at any angle, and most times his shot would be on target. He had the goal-scoring instinct of the great goal-scorer who always knows where the posts are in any situation. When he was a boy, he spent hours every day shooting against a 'goal' marked out on a wall. It is no accident that some players have a great skill which is denied others. They have worked at it from a very young age and it has not come as a gift.

Pat Holland, who joined the club a few months after me, played in the 1975 final but was not fit enough to take part in the 1980 final. Patsy is an amusing character with the East Ender's style of humour. Over the years, he has done a fine job for the club. Once after a game at Cardiff he drank the contents of a plastic container, but the 'soft drink' in it was detergent and poor Patsy ended up in hospital.

Phil Parkes played possibly his finest game for us in the first match on the trail to Wembley against WBA. But he had less to do in the replay which we won 2-1, with Geoff Pike and myself scoring the goals. Jimmy Neighbour was in the side at this time. John Lyall bought him from Norwich because he felt we needed a winger to help us get out of the Second Division. Spurs gained promotion at the first attempt by using Peter Taylor wide and John thought we would profit from similar service. It did not quite work out in our case because Jimmy took more than eighteen months to sell his house in Norwich and the commuting to London left him unsettled.

I missed the fourth round tie at Orient because of a groin strain. That was the occasion our physiotherapist Rob Jenkins used a pre-war method of treatment – a hot potato. The potato was wrapped in a sock and applied to the offending muscle. Ernie Gregory remembered this form of treatment from his early days at the club and it made a few headlines when we revived it. A hospital consultant was quoted as saying that he was surprised at a top club with access to thousands of pounds worth of equipment using such old fashioned methods, but added: 'I don't scorn it. Anything that can get heat to a groin strain is bound to do some good.'

Unfortunately the hot potatoes did not work and I had to miss the game. With Paul Brush coming in to partner Frank Lampard at full-back, Ray Stewart was moved to midfield and was our match winner in a 3-2 victory. He scored twice, once from a penalty. Ray is one of the most successful of penalty takers, another Geoff Hurst. He comes in fast and blasts the ball as hard as he can. Often the ball passes so close to the goal-keeper that if he had stayed still the ball might have been blocked. Ray operates on the theory that if you hit the ball hard enough no goalkeeper is going to stop it however badly he places his kick. Like most penalty takers, he does not practise much and rarely practises against Phil Parkes. He believes that if a goalkeeper saves from him it will affect his confidence next time he takes a penalty in a match. If he practises at all, it is in an empty net.

Tommy Taylor scored a penalty for Orient and Nigel Gray put through his own goal for our other score. Orient's Nigerian

winger John Chiedozie netted Orient's second. John has been
promoted as the new Laurie Cunningham, but he is not yet in
that class. At present I think he relies too much on speed and
service from others. In the First Division a winger needs more
than speed to be effective.

I was back for the fifth round, a hard fought 2-0 win over
Swansea City at Upton Park. Swansea's defensive system
thwarted us until near the end when Paul Allen and David Cross
scored the goals. It was just as difficult to break down Aston
Villa's defence in the sixth round. Villa had just recovered from
their boardroom battle and the upset that followed the
departures of Andy Gray and John Gidman and were emerging
into a fine young side.

A replay seemed certain until we were awarded a disputed
penalty near the end. I took a corner and as the ball swung into
the area a hand appeared from a ruck of players and tipped it
away. It certainly was not goalkeeper Jimmy Rimmer's and the
referee pointed to the spot. I could not be sure whether it was a
Villa hand or a West Ham hand, but the players nearer to the
incident appealed because they thought it was Ken
McNaught's. If I had been a Villa player I would not have been
happy about having a penalty awarded against my side. Dennis
Mortimer and his players were obviously upset although they
took the decision sportingly. Nobody envied Ray Stewart as he
stepped up to take the kick. He did not miss.

We wanted to play Everton in the semi-final, not Arsenal and
Liverpool, and that was the way the draw worked out. We were
also happy that the match was staged at Villa Park, where we
played our semi-final in 1975. Most semi-finals are taut, dour
affairs because the players do not want to lose so close to
Wembley, but this was an entertaining one. We were relieved to
see it end in a 1-1 draw as Everton took the lead and played some
good football. Their goal was highly controversial. Referee
Colin Seel of Carlisle amazed us when he blew up and signalled a
penalty as Alan Devonshire challenged an Everton player. It
was a most innocuous challenge and Dev was so upset that he
chased after the referee, remonstrating angrily. Brian Kidd,
who scored from the spot, was later sent off for kicking Ray
Stewart. I thought that too was a harsh decision.

have just swapped shirts with one of the Italian defenders at Wembley. The FA subsequently banned the exchanging of shirts on the field – they thought it was unsightly.

few caps among this group of players at a National Sporting Club function – Eddie McCredie (23 for Scotland), Cliff Jones (59 for Wales), myself, Alan Mullery (35 for England), Bobby Moore (108 for England), George Cohen (37 for England) and Alan Ball (72 for England).

For a man with a Labour background, England captain Kevin Keegan seems to getting on well with Conservative Prime Minister Margaret Thatcher! On the PM's l is Emlyn Hughes. The Prime Minister had us round to 10 Downing Street for reception before we left for the European Championship in Rome. (*Photo: Arth Edwards*)

ter a heavy night of celebrating the 1980 FA Cup Final victory, Frank Lampard and I
:d the assistance of the Mayoress of Newham to lift the trophy! (*Photo*: Monte
:sco)

friendly exchange of views with one of the Football League's outstanding referees
ve Thomas. (Well, I hope it is! I can't remember ever having upset Clive.) (*Photo*:
:ve Bacon)

The West Ham side which won the London Clubs' golf championship. I don't thin[k] contributed much with my 18 handicap! The star man of the side was Bryan 'P[op] Robson who is one of the outstanding golfer-footballers in the country. Also in [the] picture are Bobby Ferguson, Tommy Taylor, now with Orient, and John McDow[ell] who is at Norwich.

One of the most painful moments of my career. I have just accidentally headed the b[all] of an opponent's head in a match against Luton in 1974 and had to go to hospital [for] treatment on a displaced nose.

Kidd had been Everton's best attacker and it meant that he was out of the replay we had forced when Stuart Pearson, back after injury, scored the equalizer. Kidd is an unpredictable player, capable of brilliant performances and also indifferent ones. He talks a lot on the field and has been involved in a few incidents in his time. This time he was unlucky. Near the end we thought we had won when Paul Allen put the ball in the net only for the linesman to flag for offside. We could not make out who was supposed to be offside. Afterwards, I was told it was me. But I was a long way from Paul Allen and felt I could not have been interfering with play. (I seem to have heard that somewhere before!)

This is my main complaint about offside. Some referees will decide that as a player is some way away he cannot be interfering and so allow the goal. Others seem to take the interpretation of the law too literally. The element of discretion in deciding whether another player is interfering with play has to stay otherwise every time the ball is pulled back from the by-line the player making the cross would be offside when the player in the middle puts the ball into goal. But more tolerance could be shown.

Despite the controversy about Paul's 'goal' we left Villa Park in a confident frame of mind. The side that comes from behind and finishes a match well is usually in a better mental state for the replay than the one that scored first and is pegged back. The final minutes remain fresher in one's memory than the early minutes.

The replay at Elland Road was even more dramatic and entertaining than the first match. Alan Devonshire had a superb game, scoring our first goal and making a number of damaging runs down the left. Bob Latchford, in for Kidd, equalized with a near-post header in the second half to force extra time. If Bob had been a little more mobile and a little more competitive, I think he would have been England's centre-forward for years instead of being in and out of the side. He is a good player, but just a shade short of top international class.

It was appropriate that Frank Lampard should score the winner that took us to Wembley. As the excitement was reaching a peak, I took a throw, got the ball back and centred to

David Cross, who headed back towards the penalty spot. The ball went straight to Frank, who headed goalwards without too much power but with enough force to take the ball over the line on the bounce. Martin Hodge, the Everton goalkeeper, was left wrong-footed. We all wondered how Frank had managed to be up in attack and the joke in the dressing room afterwards was that he did not have enough energy to get back to his position after his previous run upfield. Frank was so overjoyed that he raced to the corner flag and did a jig round it like a South American player whose antics had been shown regularly on television that season. Frank is still embarrassed about it now.

Frank, Bill Bonds and myself were the only survivors that night from the 1975 FA Cup campaign and everyone in the club was delighted that he had made the vital contribution. Our careers had run parallel since 1967 when he made his début. He joined the club a year earlier than I had, in 1964, but we had played roughly the same number of games. Alan Taylor, now at Cambridge United after a spell in North America, was the hero of that 1975 Cup run, scoring six of our thirteen goals. They came in the last three matches – two against Arsenal in the sixth round at Highbury in his Cup début for us, two against Ipswich in a semi-final replay and two in the final against Fulham. He had scored only seven goals in fifty-five matches when Ron Greenwood signed him from Fourth Division Rochdale on 25 November 1974. The fee was £45,000, a comparatively large sum for an untried twenty-one-year-old who had cost Rochdale £3,000 from a non-League side. Alan was so frail, with thin, spindly legs, that we christened him 'Sparrow'. However he could run faster than anyone in the club, and because of his exceptional speed he was always getting injured. Defenders would stick out a leg to try to stop him and they were usually so late that they finished up catching him on the ankle. He used to be injured in training more than most players, falling on or twisting an ankle or a knee. Ron Greenwood allowed him time to settle into the club and it was not until his fourth month with us that he was given his chance in the first team. Billy Jennings, Bobby Gould and Keith Robson were the strikers when we played our first match that year in the third round at Southampton.

Lawrie McMenemy had not long taken over at the Dell and was in the process of rebuilding. We won 2-1 and were drawn at home against Swindon in the fourth round. Clyde Best was brought back for Gould but failed to take advantage of his recall. Clyde was one of the earliest of the black players and though he never said anything about it, he was hurt by the racialist chants of crowds up and down the country. He was a quiet, sensitive person and I am sure this unfair barracking affected his confidence. Speed was one of his greatest assets and he was never the same player after returning from home one summer nearly two stone overweight. He worked hard at trying to slim but never managed to get below fourteen stone. He had a gentle disposition for someone who had a Sonny Liston build and the fans kept on at him about using his physique more aggressively. However, he rarely did.

Swindon held us to a 1-1 draw and it was not one of our better displays. Peter Eastoe, now at Everton, scored their goal. Peter is a neat, compact player who has a powerful shot and good control and in those days looked good enough to play in the First Division. Swindon's most effective player, I thought, was David Moss, their winger. With more consistency he could have followed Eastoe into the First Division. In the replay at the County Ground, Swindon took the lead with a goal by Trevor Anderson. I equalized with a diving header. Although I rarely head many goals those I do all seem to come at key moments. Patsy Holland, who only played because Gould was injured and Keith Robson was suspended, scored the winner just six minutes from time.

My performance in our fifth round 2-1 success over Queens Park Rangers led one critic to write: 'Brooking simply ignored the mud and gave a display which had to be seen to be believed. He floated like a butterfly and stung like a bee, inspiring West Ham to win a superb match much more comprehensively than the score suggests.' (Certain phrases tend to dog a player's career!) We had to be sharp to beat Phil Parkes who was in goal for Rangers. I rated him in the top three or four keepers in the country in those days and a cartilage operation to his knee which still troubles him occasionally has not changed my opinion. You had to pull crosses well out of his reach because he was so adept at coming for the ball. The 'hung' cross was a waste of time against him. He does not have the build of an athlete, but there are few goalkeepers who come off their line better than he does. He made such a tremendous difference to our defence when John Lyall signed him in February 1979. Brian Clough began transforming Nottingham Forest into a good side when he signed Peter Shilton. He believes that a good goalkeeper is half the side and John Lyall felt the same way. Unfortunately, Phil's arrival at Upton Park came too late to take us up into the First Division that season.

Keith Robson, who had been at fault when Dave Clement scored the first goal for Rangers, headed the winner early in the second half. A £25,000-signing from Newcastle, Robson was one of the most skilled players on the staff at the time. He had a terrific left foot and was capable of scoring some magnificent goals. He was a determined player and had it not been for his temperament he could have become one of the leading players in the country. He was sometimes reckless on the field and even more reckless off it. He was an unmarried man when he was with us and without the security of a home base it is possible for a young player from another part of the country (he was born at Hetton-le-Hole) to get himself involved in scrapes unless he is careful. The start of his decline at the club came that season when he failed to take advice and rest a thigh injury which he had sustained in the sixth round at Highbury. That meant he missed the semi-final and the final and became very depressed as a result. Keith's problems worsened the next season when he was charged with driving while banned. Ron Greenwood went to court to speak for him, but he was found guilty. There was also the occasion when he was publicly criticized by the then chairman of the club Reg Pratt for a wild tackle in a game at Upton Park.

Though we would have preferred to have been at home against Arsenal, it was a good time to go to Highbury because there was friction within the club and the players were unhappy. Alan Ball, in particular, was most disgruntled. We were in a favourable position. No one expected us to win but Arsenal were mentally ill-prepared for the match.

The turning point came a minute before half-time. Frank

Lampard under-hit a back pass and as the ball stuck in the mud, John Radford slipped it past the oncoming Mervyn Day only to be bowled over by the keeper as he attempted to reach it. Referee Ken Burns later explained that he did not give a penalty because he thought Day went for the ball. We were leading through Alan Taylor's fifteenth minute goal and an equalizer then might have altered the course of the game.

Taylor, who had woken at six and could not get to sleep again because he was so excited about playing, was brought into the side because John Lyall thought he could exploit the slowness on the left side of the Arsenal defence. He certainly did that. Bob McNab, who was nearing the end of his career, failed to catch him and neither could Terry Mancini nor Peter Simpson.

Immediately after the interval, 'Sparrow' netted his second from my pass. It was lucky for us that Ron Greenwood had the foresight to insist that Taylor should not be Cup-tied when he signed him. It was Taylor's first full game for the club and what a game!

Alan Ball's stormy relationship with Bertie Mee was nearing its end. He later joined Southampton and had some of the happiest years of his career before becoming manager of his first club Blackpool. He found that management was no easy task even for an experienced player of his stature and soon returned to Southampton as a player. Ball had all the qualifications for a manager, but my only doubt was whether he had the tolerance needed when things go badly. He becomes incensed quickly and in management that can prove a handicap. There is a right and a wrong time to criticize. As a player, Bally had few equals. He was probably, along with Martin Peters, as good a one touch player as England have ever had. He had a fantastic game in the 1966 World Cup Final and never looked back. He was a bubbly, brash character on the field and did not change off it. I always got on well with him and enjoyed our meetings at England gatherings.

West Ham were distinctly fortunate to get past Ipswich in the semi-final and if I had been an Ipswich fan I would have been very disappointed with the outcome. Bobby Robson's team outplayed us at Villa Park in a game which ended in a 0-0 draw. It was a terrible game, as bad as any semi-final can be, with neither team wanting to push men forward in case they conceded the first goal. Already wracked by injury after playing six matches in the previous thirteen days, Ipswich had their centre-backs Kevin Beattie and Allan Hunter injured and Trevor Whymark had to move back into defence. Beattie, an England colleague, injured his knee in a hard tackle with me and after that we surprisingly lost our rhythm and never capitalized on this weakness.

In the replay at Stamford Bridge, Ipswich, without Hunter and David Johnson, again did the bulk of the attacking and had two goals disallowed. Alan Taylor scored in our first real attack in the twenty-ninth minute and again near the end when John Wark headed a clearance at him and his return shot skidded on the ice and snow and went in off a post, with Laurie Sivell beaten. Laurie is one of the smallest goalkeepers in the League at five feet seven inches, and though he is one of the bravest I felt that Ipswich were only a top goalkeeper away from being a trophy-winning side at this time. In the dressing room afterwards we were told that the Fulham v Birmingham semi-final at Maine Road had gone into extra time. We were praying that Second Division Fulham would get through. A few minutes later a steward burst into the room. 'Fulham have scored fifteen seconds from time,' he shouted. 'It's an all-London derby.'

With Bobby Moore playing out the final stages of his career at Craven Cottage, the press had a natural line to develop – Bobby versus his old mates. The *Evening Standard* brought us together for a two hour chat and we recalled a few old times. Bobby had signed for Fulham in the March of the previous year and at thirty-five years old was still a very fine player, despite losing some speed. With John Lacy, his partner, also short on pace, Ron Greenwood again had the right man for the occasion in Alan Taylor. Kevin Lock had taken Bobby's place in the West Ham side. A very quiet, unassuming lad, he had his best season for the club that year and seemed set to keep the position for many years. There are times in any player's career when he must analyze what has stopped him taking that final step to the top and in Kevin's case I felt it was his lack of ambition and absence of real determination. He was content to jog along with whatever happened. The following season a groin strain kept him out of the side and Billy Bonds was switched to his position. There was little chance of him ever getting it back and he finished up at Fulham as Bobby Moore's successor – another of football's many ironies.

Alan Mullery was the other Fulham player who monopolized the pre-match publicity. Like Moore, he was about to end a great career and the Football Writers' Association crowned it for him by voting him Footballer of the Year. The game was billed as the contest between London's two friendliest clubs. Alec Stock, Fulham's manager, was one of the most respected figures in the game. The event was also full of rarities: it was only the second all-London final; West Ham, for the second time, were the only club to field an all-English side at Wembley; and for the first time anyone could remember, the outcome was settled by two goalkeeping errors.

Peter Mellor, Fulham's Manchester-born goalkeeper, inevitably seemed confident and assured when I had seen him play previously, but on this occasion the tension of the match had affected him and his mistakes gave us the Cup in a final which was some way short of being memorable. I felt very sorry for him. If an outfield player makes a mistake he has a chance to retrieve it and people soon forget his error. But for a goalkeeper it is like a batsman out in the middle. There is little chance to recover from a mistake and much time to ponder on the consequences. Mellor's first bloomer came on the hour. Pat Holland, preferred to Bobby Gould, robbed John Cutbush and made ground on the left. His short pass inside went to Billy Jennings and as Jennings shot, Mellor failed to hold the ball. It came loose and Alan Taylor drove it back through his legs. Five minutes later, Mellor dropped Graham Paddon's shot-cum-centre from the left and again Taylor was there to punish him.

Most of my memories are about the happenings the next day. The fact that I had at last won a medal with West Ham had sunk in by then as we drove on top of a coach through the carnival-like streets of the East End. The feature writers said it was like VE Day, and not having been alive in 1945, I could not agree or disagree, but it was quite unprecedented in my experience. Without the police escort we had in 1980, it took literally hours to pass through the streets to East Ham Town Hall for the Mayor's reception. Patients were brought out of hospitals in wheel chairs to wave to us. Babies were dressed up in their prams. The noise, the colour and the excitement of it all will be an abiding memory for the rest of my life. It summed up the uniqueness of West Ham.

Ron Greenwood, who had handed over to John Lyall at the start of the season, was a notable absentee. Asked afterwards why he didn't go, he said 'It was John Lyall's day.' And of course it was. John Lyall's and everyone else's in the club, not forgetting those wonderful fans.

There are many things that need to be improved and modernized in football but the FA Cup final is not one of them. It is a worldwide occasion that has not changed for years. It is the highlight of the English football year.

8

Cup Disasters

For a side that has won the FA Cup three times in sixteen years, West Ham have also had to endure some Cup disasters sandwiched in between their triumphs in 1964, 1975 and 1980. We possessed world-class players, but still managed to go out to Third Division teams. Usually it was in a season when the club would be occupying a low position in the First Division and the FA Cup was the last competition left for us to win. Our early exit would mean that we would have nothing left to play for in the final three or four months of the season and it was frustrating for our faithful supporters.

There was no real reason for this except that there were occasions when we were guilty of failing to show resilience when the battle was going against us. I do not think the present West Ham side would have succumbed quite so easily as some earlier elevens. In the North, there was a widely held view that West Ham were 'soft', especially because we were one of the first sides to encourage players to wear gloves in freezing temperatures. Such a criticism was unjustified.

Having Bobby Moore, Geoff Hurst and Martin Peters in the side acted as a spur to our lowly opponents who invariably played above their usual form. We tried to rectify our vulnerability against inferior opposition in these one-off matches but never found it easy. One of our worst upsets came in 1967 when we were still revelling in the acclaim that followed the winning of the World Cup. We were drawn at home to Third Division Swindon in the third round and despite a hat-trick from Geoff Hurst we were held to a 3-3 draw. In the mud at County Ground, we went out 1-3 in the replay and our fans did not like it. When Bobby Moore returned to Upton Park next day, he found that the windows in his sports shop opposite had been smashed. Don Rogers, the Swindon winger, was in tremendous form at the time and he scored twenty-five goals in the League that season, a fantastic record for a winger. Don was a talented player, very quick and skilful but his attitude was too lethargic at times and he never progressed beyond the England Under-23 side. By the time he moved to Crystal Palace, it was probably too late for him to fulfill his potential. A knee injury slowed him down and he went back to Swindon. There was no doubt he could have become a full international if he had been more determined and more dedicated.

Sir Alf Ramsey and his so-called 'wingless wonders' were in vogue in the late 1960s but there were still plenty of wingers playing at the time. It is often overlooked that Ramsey had three among the twenty-two players who made up his World Cup squad in 1966 – Terry Paine of Southampton, John Connelly of Burnley and Ian Callaghan of Liverpool. They were each given a chance in 1966 before Alf adopted a 4-4-2 system.

The best winger of my time was George Best. George had everything as a footballer, even if his behaviour outside the game was open to criticism. I remember one match in my first season with the club at Old Trafford when we lost 2-4 and George scored three of the goals. It was almost a case of one man beating us on his own. I also liked the two Scots, Jimmy Johnstone, a tricky little right-winger who played at Upton Park in Bobby Moore's testimonial, and Willie Morgan who played for Manchester United and Bolton. The best English-born winger of the period was George Armstrong of Arsenal. He was three players in one – an attacking flank player who could cross the ball and also score goals, a midfield grafter and, when the other team had the ball in Arsenal's area, a full-back who could hustle and tackle as well as any defender in the side. 'Geordie' was definitely the unsung hero of the 1971 Double side.

I am all in favour of wingers. Having someone wide and getting to the by-line is one of the most productive forms of attacking play. The orthodox winger in the days of Tom Finney and Stan Matthews has been replaced by midfield players who play wide and, when their team has the ball, try to get in on the by-line. When the ball is lost, they drop back to defend. English football is so demanding that every player has to work hard. You cannot have someone like Stan Matthews waiting out on the touchline for the ball to come to him. The change of emphasis has meant that there are few specialist wingers left and I think that is a pity. England under Ron Greenwood have had some good results when Steve Coppell and Peter Barnes were playing on the flanks. Unfortunately Peter Barnes lost his confidence and form and the system had to be changed. English football benefited when these two were back together against Brazil who also played with two wingers. I hope the trend continues!

West Ham reached the fifth round of the FA Cup in 1968 after beating Burnley and Stoke away from home in the earlier rounds and there was an air of confidence at the club that this could be our year for another trip to Wembley. Unfortunately it did not survive the visit of Sheffield United and we lost 1-2 at Upton Park. United were young and inexperienced and we should not have been defeated. Tony Currie was breaking into their side at the time and so were Mick Jones and Alan Birchenall.

In 1969 we again got through the first two rounds, against Bristol City and Huddersfield, and once more our expectations were high. Our fifth-round opponents were Mansfield Town from the Third Division. The pitch was covered with snow on the Saturday and the game was postponed until mid-week. We wished it had not been because Mansfield won 3-0 and we came home in disgrace. The Mansfield fans said their side had not played as well for years. Mansfield's best player was John Quigley, the former Nottingham Forest player. It was not the first time he had played above himself against us. He seemed to make a habit of it.

In 1970 and 1971 we went out in the third round – the first year to Middlesborough and the second to Blackpool. Huddersfield knocked us out in the fifth round in 1972 which was acutely disappointing because it was a game we expected to win. Frank Worthington was in the Huddersfield side and he showed as much ability as any centre-forward of recent times.

Frank gained only eight caps for England and it should have been far more. I felt Don Revie dropped him because of his off-the-field activities, not because of what he did on the field. Frank is a fine example of the player with ability managing to stay in the game at a high level when many of his contemporaries have faded away. Trevor Cherry, another of my England team mates, was in the Huddersfield side in that match. He is a super lad as well as a fine defender. His versatility enabled him to play in a number of different positions but I thought he was at his best at centre back.

One of West Ham's most embarrassing results in the FA Cup followed in 1974 when we were beaten 1-2 in a third-round replay at Hereford. The previous year, a 1-0 defeat at Hull in the fourth round (Stuart Pearson scored the goal) had been demoralizing, but this result was far worse. We had a few inexperienced players in the side because of injury, including Alan Wooler for Bobby Moore in defence and Bertie Lutton for Bobby Gould in attack. There were enough good players to have won the match, but we could not hold an ebullient Hereford side. Dudley Tyler, who had a brief spell at Upton Park, was one of the Hereford heroes. Our FA Cup final victory over Fulham in 1975 appeared to have exorcized the Third Division hoodoo only for it to reappear in 1979 when we lost at Newport County. We gave away two sloppy goals in the mud and Mervyn Day played only one more game in the first team before the arrival of Phil Parkes from QPR.

When he first came into the side at seventeen, Ron Greenwood said Merve would be West Ham's goalkeeper for the next ten years. I remember Merve saying at the time: 'That will still only make me twenty-seven.' He had a lot of confidence for a youngster and was very mature for his age. His father died when he was young and he had become the bread winner in the family. An unaccountable decline after an initial brilliant start is not unknown with goalkeepers. As teenagers, the game comes instinctively to them and their natural ability carries them through. As they start to gain experience in the first team, they have to endure new pressures and their temperament is tested. There is no greater test than a third round of an FA Cup in front of a hostile crowd. The goalkeeper is the player closest to the fans. He has to bear most of the abuse and sometimes, even missiles. Then there are situations which test his judgment, such as when to come for crosses and when to let a defender head them away. He will be up against forwards who will try to nudge him off the ball when he is airborne. All these things are there to try him. Class goalkeepers will come through it but some falter and make mistakes as Mervyn Day did. Gary Bailey of Manchester United and John Lukic of Leeds are two present-day examples of fine young goalkeepers who went through this process. Both of them are good enough to overcome all the problems and develop into outstanding players.

One of Merve's strengths was – and still is now he has regained his confidence at Orient – coming to take crosses. He is tall, over six feet, and superbly built to withstand the hurly-burly that goes on in the six-yard box. However, in his final days at West Ham he began to make misjudgments. Several times he was caught off his line and the crowd started to barrack him. His departure was inevitable with the crowd in that mood and I am delighted he has resurrected his career at Brisbane Road.

Our heaviest FA Cup defeat in my time at West Ham came in 1978 when we went down 1-6 in a fourth-round replay at QPR. The first game was drawn 1-1 at Upton Park, Ernie Howe scoring a late equalizer. Up to half time at Loftus Road we had played so well that I said to someone in the stand (I was injured in the first game): 'We're going to win this by two or three goals.' That was the signal for an avalanche of goals . . . to the other side. Martyn Busby, playing at centre-forward for a change, scored two of them and had a particularly fine match. Stan Bowles also did well. I have always rated him one of England's most skilled players.

Derek Hales was in the West Ham side at this time, but he never settled and it was not long before he was back at Charlton. Like Ted MacDougall, he was a recognized goal-scorer who did not get too involved in build-up play. I think he would have had a more successful time with us if he had come to us first instead of starting his First Division career at Derby. West Ham had originally competed with Derby for his signature before his

£280,000 move in 1976. He had a miserable time at the Baseball Ground and by the time we signed him, he had clearly lost his appetite for the game. Possibly he had been over-priced – which is never the fault of the player – and was not allowed to forget it. Now that he is back with his first club Charlton, he is proving that he is an above-average finisher.

West Ham have not been immune to upsets in the Football League Cup too. We sunk to our lowest ebb in 1972-73 at Stockport when we lost 1-2 to a club which the following season finished ninety-second in the Football League. In 1978-79 we were defeated in the second round of the competition against our old rivals Swindon Town and what made it harder to accept was that the tie was at Upton Park. I was injured and was sent to spy on Swindon the week before. My verdict that we ought not to have too much trouble proved to be a false one, and so did my forecast that Shrewsbury, their opponents, would struggle that season. Shrewsbury were promoted. I have never been asked to report on a match since! Chris Guthrie, that much-travelled centre-forward, caused us many problems in the air and headed the winning goal in the second half. Two Swindon players who impressed me that day were Ray McHale, the midfield player who moved to Brighton and then Barnsley possibly too late in his career to make an impact in the First Division, and the defender Ken Stroud, a Londoner who played more than 200 League games for them without ever letting them down.

Eight months after our Wembley triumph against Arsenal came yet another setback, our 0-1 defeat at Wrexham in the third round of the FA Cup after a 1-1 draw at Upton Park. We had enough chances to win the first match. Twice the woodwork was struck; Paul Goddard could easily have had a hat-trick; Ray Stewart scored a hotly-contested penalty and just as we thought we had overcome some tough opponents, Gareth Davis, Wrexham's captain, volleyed in a late equalizer.

The following week we went up to Wrexham and the match was called off because of a waterlogged pitch. It was a tiring, twelve-hour day travelling there and back by coach. The match was re-arranged and again called off. By this time it was clear that the Wrexham match was going to be one of those battles we could not win. When the tie finally got under way – delaying our

League Cup semi-final against Coventry – we were below our best and a spirited rally in extra time failed to save us. Dixie McNeil, playing in defence, scored the only goal, the 222nd of his distinguished career. Once more we had an exhausting trip back in the early hours.

It was the first time the Cup holders had been knocked out in the third round since 1976. Ironically it was us who lost then 0-2 at home to Liverpool.

9

The Pass

The most important part of football is the pass. Yet in many respects it remains a neglected feature of our game. How many times are balls played up to a striker, for example, only to bounce away from him? The crowd sighs with impatience and the striker is blamed for inadequate control. But the fault is more often with the player who made the pass.

Far too many passes in English football are struck too hard. The emphasis in soccer in this country is on power and pace, and when players have been charging about at maximum speed all the time it is difficult for them to slow down and pick out a colleague with a correctly weighted pass. Many knowledgeable older supporters say there is no one in the game today who can match the passing skill of Johnny Haynes, the former Fulham and England inside-forward who was one of the finest passers of recent years. Johnny was the master of the reverse pass. He would be running one way when he would suddenly stop and hit a magnificent thirty or forty-yard ball out to the wing in the other direction. I used to go to Craven Cottage when I was a boy to watch him and even at that young age his skill left a deep impression on me.

Johnny Haynes was a great player who would stand out in any era but I maintain that if he played today, he would not hit many reverse passes! The game has changed considerably since he was in his prime. When a side loses possession today all but one or two of its players are told to get behind the ball and defend. Instead of half the team defending as in previous generations, the whole team is now defending. In these 'rush hour' conditions it is extremely hard to make accurate long passes.

There are so many players in the way, that usually the ball has to be floated over their heads.

My main aim when I receive the ball in midfield is to provide the strikers with the so called 'killer ball', the pass that puts them in with a chance of scoring a goal. With so many opponents back defending, the risk factor is high but if I can pull off two or three of these passes in a match I am doing reasonably well. If it is not possible to make a through pass, I have to make sure we keep possession by finding a colleague. Success in finding the target often depends on movement, with the aim being to play a ball into space at the same time a forward arrives to receive it. The passer will want to 'weight' the ball so that the receiver can control it easily. He will prefer it dropping at his feet so that the defender behind him cannot get the ball off him.

Ron Greenwood had a favourite expression 'always make sure you've got pictures in your mind'. He meant that you should have an impression of where the other players were standing before the ball reached you so that you could react accordingly. If a defender is tight and someone nearby is free, then a first time pass is the obvious choice.

Usually when the ball is coming in my direction, I will glance behind me to see who is there. I can do this because I am fairly confident that I can still control the ball although I have taken my eye off it. Some players cannot do this. They feel they need to give all their attention to the ball. My control is good because I spent so much time trapping balls bouncing off walls, drainpipes and ledges when I was a boy. It is like learning to read or learning to type. It is a skill that never leaves you.

Another piece of advice which Ron Greenwood gave us as youngsters was to receive the ball sideways on. If you are square on to the ball your vision is restricted to the direction the ball has just come from, but by standing sideways half the field is open to you and the passing opportunities are much greater. Something else he encouraged us to do was to let the ball run as it came to us and run with it. I do this a lot although it needs a pass which is properly weighted, and first I have to check that there is no defender in the way.

These good habits are extremely useful to have in the struggle against persistent defenders. In my time in the game, creative players are given less time and space than when I made my first team début. I do not object to the increased pace because if players are rushing about, it will mean that defenders are more likely to dive in. If they commit themselves, I have a better chance of beating them.

Ron Greenwood always encouraged players to take on opponents and that is another habit which has never left me. At West Ham we have players all over the field who can take the ball past defenders. Not many sides have a player as adroit as Alan Devonshire in making telling runs. I think he could finish up as England's left-side flank player because he has the ability to make a winger's cross as well as perform as a midfield player.

Enzo Bearzot, the Italian manager, once said of me: 'Like Johan Cruyff, he is deceptive, yet so perceptive. It is not his pace, as much as his change of pace, that makes him so difficult to mark.' A change of pace, a change of direction, are essentials in my game. If I have the ball I have the advantage over a defender because I make the first move. I believe our game would improve if the pace we play it at was reduced. Players would then have the time to make better use of their skills. But with so much importance attached to winning the likelihood of this happening is small. Our winning sides are those that are well organized and work tirelessly. Nottingham Forest were a good example when they came out of the Second Division. They overran opponents. They were a typically English-style team. Aston Villa are perhaps the best example from today's teams – young, superbly fit and enthusiastic. Arsenal's Brian Talbot is a fine example of the English power player, a man who never stops running. West Bromwich Albion's Bryan Robson is another all-action midfield player. There are more players of this type than the old-fashioned 'touch' players. Ipswich, with Dutchmen Frans Thijssen and Arnold Muhren, have sought to mould styles towards a more delicate approach, but few teams show signs of copying them. Both Thijssen and Muhren have a feel for the ball. When they pass it, they make certain the weight is right, and they will bend a ball round an opponent if it is necessary.

Liverpool are perhaps the leading exponents of a power game

based on good passing methods. When Ray Clemence throws the ball out to a defender, it will usually be a full-back who has gone wide, and either Phil Neal or Alan Kennedy will be content to play the ball square to Alan Hansen or Phil Thompson in the middle if the opportunity of a forward pass does not arise. They can afford to play this way because they win many more games than they lose. If a team near the bottom did it, the fans would soon be shouting at them. Hansen is one of the best passers in our game and has developed into an outstanding player. As he is very often the spare man at the back, he is able to go off on runs in the Franz Beckenbauer manner. Not many players in England have the confidence to do that.

Beckenbauer is probably the finest ever all-round passer, a master of both the short and long ball with either foot. It is rare that a player is equally adept at executing these passes. Alan Ball is brilliant at the short game and few players have matched his one touch play in neat triangles with colleagues. Two of the best long passers in recent years were Bobby Moore and Bobby Charlton. Bobby Moore's service to his front men was so near perfect that the receiver needed little time to control the ball. Charlton personified the attacking midfield player, and was capable of reaching colleagues with sweeping twenty- or thirty-yard passes with both feet. Only Tony Currie in the modern game has come near to matching his long-range accuracy. Unlike Currie, Charlton had the good fortune to keep clear of injury. Curiously, many of the greatest players, Charlton, George Best, Billy Wright, Tom Finney, Stan Matthews and Bobby Moore among them, were able to play out their careers without being seriously injured.

Perhaps the closest to a Bobby Charlton today is Ray Wilkins, his successor in the Manchester United midfield. Ray's range of passes is superior to most other midfield players, and he has the ability to strike the ball at the right pace. The number of full-backs who can be relied upon for accurate service has declined, but there are some who are carrying on the tradition of George Cohen, Ray Wilson and Terry Cooper. I like Aston Villa's Kenny Swain, who used to be a right-winger when at Chelsea. Liverpool-born Kenny has become one of the best attacking right-backs in the country. His passing skills are those of a high-class forward. Kenny Samson, Viv Anderson, Frank Gray and Danny McGrain are all examples of full backs who can excite crowds with their attacking surges.

Out of sixteen years and more than 550 games of professional football, it is hard for me to pick out passes which I think have surpassed any other in my career. I recollect the one-two with Kevin Keegan against Scotland at Wembley as an example of a short pass. The wall pass is so simple yet it is difficult to execute well. In theory hitting the ball against a colleague so that it comes back in the direction of your run seems fairly easy, but there are so many factors working against it. The pace of the ball has to be right. The angle has to be right. The run of the receiver has to be timed perfectly. That day, I felt, Kevin and I achieved near perfection.

A long pass which pleased me immensely was the cross which I put over at Newcastle some years ago for Ted MacDougall to dive and head a goal. I took possession of the ball on the right, beat Frank Clarke, and had time to look up before driving the ball beyond the penalty spot towards MacDougall. 'Pop' Robson had gone to the near post, taking a defender with him and his part in the goal was probably overlooked by nearly everyone except the players. Yet his part was almost as important as mine, or Ted MacDougall's.

In those days I often drifted towards the wings and carried out the role of a winger. In the past two years, however, I have been able to get into the box and score more goals. The team has become stronger all round and other players like Devonshire, Geoff Pike and Patsy Holland have been able to get in on the by-line.

English players are frequently criticized for not being capable of matching the Continentals in their skill at bending the ball. Partly this is because it is hard to put purchase on the ball when you are under pressure and being harassed. There are, however, some players who can do it very effectively. Glenn Hoddle is perhaps the best example. He has a great feel for the ball and can bend it with either foot. When I kick with my left foot, I usually bend the ball from left to right involuntarily. The ball curls like an inswinger to a right-handed batsman. I find I wrap my foot round the ball producing a swinging effect which does not occur when I am kicking with my right foot. I think most left-footed players can bend the ball more than a right-footed player. With me, it is probably a legacy of my years of training to become two-footed. My left, being the weaker foot, struck the ball in a different way to my right. When I take my boots off, the left one is curled inwards more than my right. Liam Brady, the best left-footed passer in the British game until he went to Juventus, also tends to curl the balls in with his left foot.

Brady is a player who uses a change of pace to shake off defenders and I feel that since his departure Arsenal's game has become more frantic. Speed of thought is more important than speed of action. No one could say Bobby Moore or Emlyn Hughes were the fastest movers on the football field but they more than made up for any apparent slowness with the way they anticipated events. Colin Todd was another back-four defender who had this gift of quick reactions. But Toddy was a quick mover as well. I cannot remember many times when he went for a tackle and failed to take the ball.

Any discussion about passing and controlling the ball has to take into account the pressure put on the players concerned by the opposition. It has to be accepted that the English game is more aggressive than most styles of football played round the world. On the Continent, midfield players will drop off and let the opposition advance into their half unchallenged. This makes it easier to build up and work the ball. In England, you can be challenged all over the field and when one player is beaten, there is usually another one waiting behind him to get in a tackle.

I think the game has become more physical in my time in it. The worst example of violent tackles can still be seen in the Italian League, whereas here most of the horrific ones have been outlawed. Week in and week out, however, there are probably more hefty challenges going on in an average First Division match here than in any other comparable League. Defenders will 'test' a forward in the opening minutes with an illegal challenge. If the referee fails to pick it up, they will try it again, and again. The onus is very much on the referee to control such incidents. A strong, brave referee will step in straight away, in the first minute if necessary. A compromising referee will let it go and probably find the game running away from him later. It is still true that some managers will instruct defenders to try and soften up a particular opponent. I am sure Orient's opponents are told this sometimes because Orient's Nigerian winger John Chiedozie is a particular type of player who can attract 'the treatment'.

Some players who are looked on as individualists, such as Stan Bowles or Trevor Francis, can find themselves being chopped down. Crowd-pleasing players are lucky if they escape a heavy challenge at some time in a game whether fair or foul. I can see no way of stopping this. Not every referee sees an incident the same way.

Strikers will always be prime targets, and until the tackle from behind is banned they will continue to be injured. Outlawing this type of tackle is not so simple because, as Ken Aston and his refereeing colleagues have demonstrated, it is possible to tackle an opponent from the rear and not commit an offence. What needs to be eradicated is the tackle through the opponent. There are still too many of these in our game and the forward is left in a heap on the ground. His assailant will claim that he got the ball, but he also got the man.

The head as well as the feet can be used to pass a ball. And few players have surpassed the skill of Geoff Hurst at flicking the ball on with his head. Certainly no one has bettered him in his ability to use the chest as a means of passing the ball. Joe Royle in his prime was also good at these skills, and two players who impress me today are Peter Withe of Aston Villa and Paul Mariner of Ipswich. Perhaps the best player at this is Arsenal's Frank Stapleton, who with Paul Mariner comes closest of modern players to fulfilling the many requirements of an all-round striker.

10

Playing for Alf, Don, Joe and Ron

In seven years as an England player, I have played under four managers. The first, Alf Ramsey, was similar in many ways to the fourth, Ron Greenwood. They were contemporaries as players and believed in a relaxed, friendly atmosphere at England gatherings. They treated the players with courtesy and respect, and with almost paternal concern from Ramsey. There was nothing Ramsey would not do for his players. Everyone liked him and I have yet to hear one of his former players criticize him as a person. I only travelled abroad once under him, when I made my début in Lisbon on a rainy day in April 1974, and I was impressed with the way he fussed over us. He could have been trying to curry favour with the members of the FA International Committee who were at that time debating his future but instead he spent his time with the players. I had first met him in the Under-23 side in 1972 – I scored against Switzerland with a header in one game at Ipswich – and then had been called up for the senior squad for the Austria, Poland and Italy games in 1973.

When selected for the England squad, Ted Croker, the FA secretary, writes a letter to say you have been picked, but few players receive the news by letter. Their club manager, who has been told in advance, usually breaks the news, or you hear it on the radio. Ron Greenwood told me of my selection. It signifies the peak of a footballer's career and that he is in the top sixteen out of 2,000 or more professional footballers who are eligible in the country. To prove this he receives a lightish-blue velvet cap with silver quartering and a tassel. Some players give their caps away or toss them into a drawer but I have kept all mine – now nearing fifty – in my display cabinet. Each one is embossed with the details of the match.

When I arrived for the get-together before the Austria match, Ramsey shook my hand and warmly remarked: 'Welcome, I hope you enjoy yourself with us. The others lads will make you feel at home. There is a good spirit here. I hope it goes well for you.' His public image was of a dour, uncommunicative man, yet it did not tally with my first impression of him. Nothing that happened later changed my opinion. He never said anything negative about how he wanted the team to play. The emphasis was on going forward, not stopping opponents. Ramsey had a passion about passing. A good passer himself when he was a player, he hated seeing players giving the ball away. 'Treat the ball like a precious jewel,' he would say. It was a sentiment I agreed with entirely.

England hit a peak that September night against Austria, scoring seven goals without reply. The Austrian manager Leopold Stasny commented afterwards that England could still teach the world how to play. Almost every chance seemed to go in and it was a good augury for our World Cup qualifying match against Poland at Wembley three weeks later. Mike Channon scored twice from the right, Allan Clarke also got a couple and Martin Chivers, playing alongside Clarke, Tony Currie and Colin Bell each scored once. It was a very attacking side with all three midfield players, Currie, Bell, included in preference to the ball-winning Peter Storey, and Peters, considerable goal-scorers in their own right.

All the elation, however, disappeared after that disastrous match against Poland. The Poles 1-1 draw was enough to keep us out of the World Cup finals in West Germany the following year and the press and public could not accept that we had failed. There had to be a scapegoat and it was Ramsey. He told the players afterwards: 'You couldn't have done more. I'm sorry you're not going. Pick up your heads. Let me do the worrying.' As he had done so often before, he did not blame the players or lambast anyone for making mistakes. Norman Hunter's error on the halfway line which led to Domarski's goal had proved calamitous, yet he never criticized Norman in public. Norman stalked round the silent dressing room uttering angrily: 'I should have clattered him into touch.' He got changed quickly and rushed off to drive home to Leeds through the night.

It was universally agreed that Alf's lack of rapport with the press helped in his downfall. He treated everyone the same and was polite and answered any reasonable questions. But he revealed little of his innermost thoughts. He was the shield between the players and the outside world. I never saw him really angry or swear or lose his temper. If he was upset about something, his voice would continue to be well modulated and precise, but the tone hardened. He was like a kettle just about to boil with the lid firmly in place. Recognizing the need to convert public opinion, Don Revie did not make the same mistake. He went out of his way to cultivate the press, laying on drinks and sandwiches for his meetings with them whereas Ramsey had left them to their own devices. I remember Revie telling us: 'The press have a job to do and are going to do it regardless whether you assist them or not. You should put yourselves out to help them. If you are polite and helpful they're going to be more behind you than against you.' There were some players, notably Kevin Keegan, who felt Revie's help to the reporters went too far. Kevin said one or two reporters were told more than the players themselves and that was not good for team spirit. Revie's policy, in the main, worked. Despite all the changes and the poor results, England received less criticism than in the Ramsey days when the team was more successful.

Ramsey had built England's best-ever side, in terms of results, in 1966, and his 1970 side was possibly even better in terms of football ability. The way we went out of the World Cup competition 2-3 to West Germany in Leon after leading 2-0 was almost like a Greek tragedy. I believe it turned Ramsey against using substitutes. England had the match won until Ramsey took Bobby Charlton and Martin Peters off to save their legs for the next game, replacing them with Norman Hunter and Colin Bell. At the time it looked a sensible move, but it backfired and Ramsey was never allowed to forget it.

As the Polish match in 1974 reached its frantic climax at Wembley, with England failing to score from thirty-four goal attempts (the goal in the 1-1 draw came from a penalty taken by

Allan Clarke) and also failing to profit from twenty-three corners, Bobby Moore, sitting with me on the bench, tried to persuade Ramsey to put on a substitute in the second half.

'It's getting desperate Alf (all the players called Sir Alf 'Alf', even the junior ones),' he said. 'Don't you think it would be a good idea to get a left-sided player on?' Ramsy replied: 'I've pushed Norman forward on that side.' Moore tried again. 'It's too late,' said Ramsey. The crowd were yelling for new blood. 'Stick a left sided player on, Alf,' said Moore. 'We might get them down that side. It's never too late. Get Kevin Hector on for two minutes and see what he can do.'

Two minutes from time Ramsey relented. 'Kevin, get changed,' he said.

Ray Clemence, thinking he meant Kevin Keegan, started to undress him, whipping his shorts and under pants down to his knees. Hector got on, in place of Martin Chivers, and almost scored with his only kick in his ninety seconds of action. Hector, a fine clubman with Derby, played once more for England, again only as a substitute.

The squad for the trip to Portugal the following year was weakened by injury and FA Cup replays and one of those left out was Peter Osgood, who was recalled after a four-year gap to play against Italy a month after the Polish upset. That had been Osgood's fourth and final cap. Highly talented, he had not done his ability justice. Stan Bowles was the new striker. Stan made an immediate impact with Alf. Every time Alf gave an instruction, he said: 'That all right with you, Stan?'

Martin Peters was the new captain and there were six new caps, including Phil Parkes. It was Phil's sole England cap. He has been called up many times but with Ray Clemence and Peter Shilton around, he has never been able to break into the side again. It was also Dave Watson's début. A late developer, Dave has single-mindedly made himself into one of Europe's best defenders. He brings his own portable music equipment along to every England gathering and if you share a room with him you have to be a rock fan. He has it on all the time. Steve Coppell had only a passing interest in rock when he first shared a room with him and now he is a convert.

Alf was upset before the Portugal game at the large number of withdrawals from the squad. He felt that there was only one thing to do, and that was to punish the clubs concerned. If a player did not report for an international or a training session, he should not be permitted to play for his club on the following Saturday. Two of the players who dropped out were Paul Madeley and Norman Hunter from Leeds. During the final years of Ramsey's reign, Leeds under Don Revie had more players dropping out of international squads than possibly any other club. Madeley replied to Ramsey, saying: 'Sir Alf once told me that unless I was one hundred per cent fit I should drop out of the squad. Who would be foolish enough to pass up a chance of earning £100?' The problem of club commitments clashing with international matches has been and always will be a hindrance to a successful national side. Only a reduction in club fixtures will remedy this.

Although I enjoyed the match itself, the result, a 0-0 draw, was not very inspiring. The Portuguese also had a makeshift team out and what with the rain and the political climate, it was a dull trip. A miserable exit, in fact, for Alf Ramsey. The players had no inkling of it at the time, but that was his last match in charge. Four weeks later Ramsey was sacked by the FA who issued a statement:

Following meetings, a unanimous recommendation was submitted to the executive committee that Sir Alf Ramsey should be replaced as England team manager. A new manager will be appointed in due course. In view of the forthcoming international matches in the Home Championship, against the Argentine and a three-match European tour, it was decided that a caretaker manager should be appointed. With the approval of Coventry City, Mr Joe Mercer has agreed to undertake this task. It should be stated that he does not wish to be considered for the post of permanent manager so immediate steps will be taken to appoint a new manager as soon as possible. The FA wishes at this time to record its deep appreciation for all that Sir Alf has accomplished and the debt owed to him by English football for his unbending loyalty and dedication and the high level of integrity he has brought to world football.

Under Ramsey, England played 113 matches, winning 69 and losing 17. Typically, Alf did not comment to the press. He was away on holiday at the time. When he returned he could have made a lot of money selling his story to one of the Sunday papers. He kept his own counsel, retiring to his home in Ipswich and politely turning inquiring pressmen away. A few years later, he was quoted as saying: 'No one cares about me any more, only my wife and my dog.' It was all very sad.

The new regime under Joe Mercer was the opposite – a laugh a minute. One of life's truly happy men, Joe had a funny line for every situation. 'Team talk,' he would say, 'what do we want one of those for?' His meetings used to last about two minutes: 'I don't know much about this other lot. Let's not worry about them. Let them worry about us.' He had a habit of either getting the players' names mixed up, forgetting their names altogether or mispronouncing them. Roy McFarland, for example, was McParland. Although there was a light-headed atmosphere, it never became frivolous. Les Cocker remained from the Ramsey era – a permanent feature of the England set-up. I remained in the squad, but was apprehensive about my position because Joe included Keith Weller, the Leicester midfield player who had failed to gain a cap under Ramsey in all three Home Championship matches.

Keith came from Islington and had a typical lively Cockney attitude to life. At Millwall he was very successful in partnership with Derek Possee, another former Spurs player. But his best football was played at Leicester and he was especially good at going on runs and beating opponents. He is probably best known for being one of the first players to wear tights in a Football League match – it took some courage to do that but Keith never lacked courage.

From being an accepted member of the party, I now thought my international career was about to be cut short, especially as Weller scored the only goal against Northern Ireland. But events turned in my favour. McFarland sustained an Achilles tendon injury in the Irish match which kept him out of the game for six months and Stan Bowles walked out the following day in disgust at not having been picked. There were now some vacancies in the side. I filled one of them against the Argentine on the Wednesday after the 0-2 defeat against the Scots at Hampden Park. I played on the left side in midfield alongside Weller and Colin Bell but I probably would not have played if England had won on the Saturday. The Argentinians were typically South American, good on the ball and excellent passers. A young player named Kempes scored both goals, including a late penalty. However, I was more impressed by the long-haired striker Ayala. It was the Argentine's first visit to Wembley since 1966 when Alf Ramsey called them animals. It made some of us wonder about the timing of Alf's sacking. There could have been some embarrassment if he had still been in charge. The only incident this time came at the end of the match when Emlyn Hughes was involved in a slight scuffle with Glaria.

The England tour to East Germany, Bulgaria and Yugoslavia was a daunting prospect which was made lighter by the atmosphere engendered by Joe Mercer. It was originally planned as a warm up for the 1974 World Cup but as England had already been knocked out it served no worthwhile purpose, especially as a new England manager was due to be appointed and who might well have ideas totally different to those of Ramsey and Mercer. Joe's good nature and joviality prevented it becoming a depressing trip which it could easily have been under someone else. His theme was 'enjoy yourself' and if a player wanted to go out for a drink, Joe did not prevent him. And when it was a matter of someone going for a lie down and a rest it was usually Joe himself who went, to ease his back. He really excelled in Belgrade, where the third and final match was played on 5 June 1974.

While we were waiting for the usual formalities to be gone through at the airport on arrival, Kevin Keegan sat on the luggage conveyor belt. Suddenly it was switched on and the airport police were under the impression that Keegan was fooling about. They jumped on him and marched him to a room where he said later he had been kicked and assaulted. The rest of the players were so angry when they found out that they wanted to catch the next flight back to London. 'We can all go home, no problem,' said Joe, 'but Kevin won't be able to come with us. He'll have to stay and answer any charges. The only

way we'll get him out is by sticking together and answering
them on the field. It's their country off the field, but they can't
stop us on it.' His speech won us over and after further talks
involving Emlyn Hughes, the captain, and the FA officials, it
was decided to go ahead with the game after lodging a formal
complaint about the treatment meted out to Kevin.

It was therefore fitting that Kevin should head the equalizer
in a 2-2 draw. The Yugoslavs had some fine players in their side,
including Oblak and Surjak, and two who finished up with
English clubs, Acimovic, who scored for Sheffield Wednesday
six years later at Upton Park, and Mucinic, who went to
Norwich City. Despite my fears about being unwanted, I
played in all three matches, the 1-1 draw in East Germany, the
1-0 victory in Bulgaria and the match in Belgrade.

Kevin was just emerging as an established international
player. I did not see him then as a world star. That only came
when he had the courage to leave English football and play
abroad. His spell with SV Hamburg changed him from a very
good, hard working player into 'European Footballer of the
Year' on two occasions and his success has encouraged a few
more English players to play abroad. I have often been called a
Continental-type player myself, preferring to try to use the ball
creatively instead of fighting for it, but it is too late now for me
to think of moving. If I had been ambitious to play abroad I
would have followed Kevin's example and gone to West
Germany, where the football would suit me better than in Italy
or Spain. In Italy you never know whether you are about to be
kidnapped and Spanish football tends to be too physical.

It would be bad for our game if too many good players went
abroad. I think the balance is about right at the moment with
only a handful of players such as Tony Woodcock, Liam Brady
and Laurie Cunningham with foreign clubs. There has been an
exchange of players inside Europe for years and it makes sense
that our footballers should mix in as well. One of the chief
reasons for our recent decline is that we are too self-contained,
too oblivious to what is happening outside the British Isles. It is
a sign of our insularity that there are no top foreign coaches
working in the Football League. Our football would benefit
from new ideas but our system of play is so entrenched that I can

see immense difficulties if a club decided to appoint a foreigner.

When the party arrived home, the talk was about who would succeed Alf Ramsey. Joe's spell as caretaker had ended. Most of us felt that Don Revie was the natural choice. Leeds had just won the League Championship by five points from Liverpool and in his time at Elland Road, Leeds had won the FA Cup, the Football League Cup and the Inter-City Fairs Cup (before it became the UEFA Cup) besides being finalists in the European Cup. Revie was the most successful club manager in England and a clear favourite for the post. The players mostly thought he was the man for the job. I do not remember anyone saying anything about Leeds being responsible for introducing so-called professionalism and cynicism into the game and that this should be held against Revie. Nor did anyone at the FA raise the subject of the many withdrawals of Leeds players from England squads, or the Leeds' disciplinary record. Leeds started the 1973-74 season under threat of a £3,000 fine imposed by the FA because their total of sendings off and cautions had risen above an acceptable level. The fine was to be implemented if there was no improvement but there was a significant drop in the number of offences so the penalty was never imposed.

Revie was appointed on 3 July 1974. One of his first moves was to hold a mass meeting of eighty current and potential England players in Manchester to outline what he wanted. I thought that was a good move. It was telling the fringe players that they were in his thoughts and it stimulated competition to get into the England squad.

Revie soon struck me as being outwardly less of a strong personality than Ramsey. He was quiet and methodical and put his views over in typically Yorkshire forthright manner without being demonstrative. He said England had slipped back in the ratings and he wanted to see us climb the ladder again in time for the 1978 World Cup. The basis of his appeal was patriotism. We were going to do it for the fans and for the country and it came as no surprise later when he adopted 'Land of Hope and Glory' as England's anthem. We had our own tune within the camp, 'It's a Grand Old Team to Play for'. Revie tried to create the togetherness he had built up at Leeds. He was desperate to succeed and passionately wanted the England team to be back as Number One in the world. In the end, and this was possibly why he failed, he tried too hard.

Things soon changed from the Ramsey relaxed approach. There was a curfew, and the night before a match we had to be in our rooms by ten o'clock. Les Cocker, appointed as his assistant, used to visit the rooms to make sure we were all in and asked us if we wanted anything. Some players cannot sleep before games and ask for a sleeping tablet. I have steered clear of sedatives. I usually sleep well before games and badly after them because I play the match through time and time again in my head like a record. But that does not matter as there is no match the next day. Under Ramsey, there was an arrangement that players had to be in bed by eleven o'clock before games, but there was an easy going approach on other days.

Revie was ridiculed in some quarters for introducing bingo sessions and carpet bowls, but I did not think these attempts to bring the squad together were bad ideas. The trouble with being away on England trips is that the players get a lot of free time which they do not know how to fill except by playing cards, reading or listening to music. Having so much free time leads to a bored, casual air and I must admit this has affected me when I have been abroad. Being too relaxed in the build up can reduce motivation in matches. I need to have something to occupy my time because when I am busy, I play better.

Don Revie's famed dossiers were the opposite of the Mercer style of letting the opposition worry about us. We were now cast in the position of having to worry about the opposition, and it may have proved psychologically harmful for some players. Revie and his staff compiled a record of every opponent which we were expected to study the night before matches. There were some usful bits of information such as where the other team put their defenders at corners, how they took their free kicks and who tended to go where. But reading that one's immediate opponent had 'a great left foot' and could do this and that was not conducive to inspiring confidence.

Revie was a great one for meetings. He would ask the players for their views but the pattern was usually the same. One or two of the senior players such as Mike Channon or Alan Ball would contribute, but the rest would sit in silence. I cannot remember

West Ham's 1975 FA Cup Final triumph is celebrated by some of our fans. Long sideburns were fashionable in those days! (*Photo*: Sporting Pictures)

ιe hunter hunted. I am trying to take the ball off Tommy Smith, the former Liverpool
;ht back, in the England v Team America friendly in 1976. I don't think I succeeded!
hoto: Monte Fresco)

West Ham's FA Cup winning squad. Left to right: (back) Phil Parkes, myself, Bill Bonds, Alvin Martin, Pat Holland, Jimmy Neighbour, Paul Brush, Bobby Ferguson (Front) David Cross, Stuart Pearson, Alan Devonshire, Paul Allen, Ray Stewart, George Pike and Frank Lampard. (*Photo*: Central Press)

Trevor Brooking the businessman. I am just about to leave home for a morning's work at the office of Colbrook Plastics where I am the financial director. When I eventually retire from football I will go into business full-time. Football management with its insecurities isn't for me! (*Photo* Reg Lancaster)

hough I hold an FA Full Badge as a coach and enjoy coaching very much, I certainly
ll not make it my career after I give up playing football. (*Photo*: Monte Fresco)

One of my rare near-post headers, Geoff Hurst style! The victims are Watford defend[er] Ian Bolton and goalkeeper Eric Steele in a Second Division match at Upton Park.

In pursuit of that fi[rst?] Brazilian midfield play[er] Zico during England's 0[–1?] defeat against Brazil in t[he] US Bicentennial Tourn[a]ment in 1976. (*Photo*: Mon[ty] Fresco)

anyone disagreeing with him. He introduced bonuses for winning and losing on top of the £100 appearance money which had not changed for years. This was well-received by the players, especially as bonuses were commonplace at clubs. No one was going to play any harder because of the money. The glory of playing for England was enough motivation.

Whereas Alf Ramsey had possibly been too loyal to players and kept some on when they should have been left out, Revie went the other way. He kept chopping and changing the side. Seven changes for one match. Seven changes in the next. There was no stability and no pattern. He was ruthless enough to make the changes but not far-seeing enough to realize that a blend would only come if a side was selected from the same fifteen or sixteen players. I was one of the first to go, and in the year I was out of the team he used twenty-two players, two whole teams. He judged everything on the result. If we failed to win, he would try more players. Personally, I felt he took too much notice of the press and bowed too easily to public opinion.

He told me off at half time in his second match, against Portugal at Wembley on 20 November 1974. 'Stay on that right side,' he said. 'You are unbalancing the team by drifting over to the left.' I was amazed. At West Ham under Ron Greenwood I had been taught that one of the essentials of the game was space and how to use it. I had been encouraged to find space wherever it was. Now I was being tied down to a more rigid pattern of play. Just over two years later Johan Cruyff and the Holland side came to Wembley and showed us all about space and how it should be exploited. That 0-2 defeat by Holland was the lowest level England's team reached under Revie. It signalled the beginning of the end for him.

England were booed off the pitch after the 0-0 draw against Portugal, but it had not been like that after Revie's first game a month earlier against Czechoslovakia at Wembley. We left the field, 3-0 victors, to cheers and 'God Save Our Glorious Team'. England's players were in their new Admiral strip of red and blue stripes down the arms and the 86,000 crowd were given 'Land of Hope and Glory' song sheets to help whip up the national fervour. I was on the bench, which confirmed my fears that Revie was more defensive in outlook than Ramsey, and as an attacking player I was much less likely to figure in his long term plans. However, with twenty minutes to go it was still 0-0 when Revie showed that his attitude towards substitutions was going to be much different from Ramsey's. He asked me to replace Martin Dobson on the right in midfield and Dave Thomas to go wide on the left for Frank Worthington. Thomas, a very quiet person, was probably the leading winger in the country about this time. He had pace and the ability to cross a good ball but lacked consistency. He was one of a procession of players tried by Revie who could not bridge the gap between club and international football. Two minutes after we came on Channon headed in a cross from Thomas and that was the breakthrough. Colin Bell scored twice more in nine minutes and what had been a tight game ended in a comfortable 3-0 win to start off our European Championship campaign.

Being substituted can be one of the more unpleasant things that happens to an international player and it happened to me two years later during the World Cup qualifier against Finland at Wembley which saw us scramble a 2-1 win against a team of amateurs. I was about to take a corner on the far side when I saw the trainer come out with the number '10'. It was the worst possible time for it to happen because it meant I had to trot back across the pitch. And I was more disappointed because Hilkka, my number one fan was watching, and we were playing against her countrymen. I was even more surprised when I saw that my replacement was a defender, Mick Mills. Revie was using a 4-2-4 formation in an effort to run up a big score against the weakest opponents in the group. Goal difference, he thought, could be the difference between qualifying and not qualifying. As it turned out, he was right.

Ray Wilkins and I had been over-run several times when the Finns broke from defence and Revie feared that they might snatch a goal. 'I want someone to sit in and hold it on that side,' he said. Surprisingly, considering the quality of the opposition, there was a crowd of 98,000 at Wembley that night. By the end they were chanting 'What a load of rubbish'. Revie's expert handling of the public relations side meant that we were attracting much bigger crowds than in the Ramsey era.

After the disappointment against Portugal, I was left out of the next match, a friendly against West Germany at Wembley. Alan Ball was reinstated as captain, a shrewd move in view of his contribution to winning the World Cup in 1966. Emlyn Hughes made way for him and a newcomer, Alan Hudson, was brought in to midfield. His performance on a sodden pitch was highly praised by the critics. West Germany's 2-0 defeat was their first since winning the World Cup the year before. Malcom Macdonald scored one of the goals and in an European Championship match a month later set a record by scoring all five in the 5-0 rout of Cyprus. Hudson had all the qualities needed, on the field at least, to be an international player but I did not feel Macdonald had. I just thought there were too many players given a chance by Revie. These needless experiments hampered progress towards building a good, all-round side. The best players, or whoever Revie thought were the best players, should have been kept together for four or five matches. But it never happened. Four changes were made for the return trip to Cyprus, where we scored a disappointing 1-0 victory, and more new faces were introduced for the Home Championship including Colin Viljoen of Ipswich, another rival to me in midfield. Gerry Francis was also back after injury and his part in the 5-1 win over the Scots at Wembley seemed certain to make him one of Revie's key players for the next few years. Gerry had the all-round skills needed for the job and only his fitness let him down. Revie showed his confidence in him by making him captain and jettisoning Ball. I felt that Ball was left out too soon. He was still one of the top midfield players in the country. Maybe it was a personality clash. Hudson, too, had gone.

It has been said that Revie got rid of all the rebels and only kept in the good guys but that is not in keeping with his record at Leeds, or in his early days with England. Kevin Keegan and Kevin Beattie both walked out of England squads and were forgiven by Revie. He had this fatherly way with players that led to his nickname 'The Godfather'.

In June of that summer he invited thirty players to the West Park Lodge – the hideaway country hotel he had discovered near Potters Bar, north of London – for a get-together, and to my delight, I was one of them. He took me into his room and in a private talk told me I could be a regular member of his side if I ironed out some faults. He thought I should be more aggressive and try to dictate play more than I did. 'Midfield is the most important part of the team,' he said. 'That's where it all starts. You've got a tendency to drift out of games. You drift along with the game instead of shaping it the way you want it.' I accepted his well-meaning advice. It was true that I could have been more assertive. Since then, I think I have improved in that respect. I hope so.

My exile from the team lasted one day short of a year. On 19 November 1975, I was brought back for the return game against Portugal in the Sporting Lisbon Stadium. The Portuguese have had a habit of appearing in my international story. My first international was against them and so was my last game before my year's break.

This match was no different from the previous ones. It was dull and uninspiring with a spectacular free kick from defender Rodrigues beating Ray Clemence to put the home side ahead. Mike Channon equalized to make the final score 1-1. That result meant we were virtually out of the European Championship and the inquests started. Don Revie tried to divert some of the criticism by suggesting that our preparation was inadequate. He argued that England needed a free Saturday before midweek internationals to give them a fair chance to compete with opponents who had far more time to prepare. Alan Hardaker, secretary of the Football League, responded angrily. In a personal attack on Revie, he said: 'It wouldn't have made a scrap of difference to England's performance in Lisbon if League matches had been postponed. We smacked of excuses before we left for Portual. At present it is money, money, money.' I sided with Revie over this issue. Our preparation was inadequate and it was untrue and unfair to claim that the England players were only motivated by money.

Revie was criticized for involving the England team in commercial deals, including the shirt deal with Admiral, but I felt the criticism was unnecessary. The income from these sources went into FA funds and was distributed at lower levels in the game to help improve standards and facilities. Bisham Abbey and Lilleshall, the two main coaching centres for football in England, have been supported with money from commercial projects and FA coaching courses have benefited. If extra revenue had not been raised, the number of FA coaches working full-time would not be as high as it is now. Revie's critics overlook these points. They also ignore the fact that nearly every Football League club in the country now has a commercial section and in many cases clubs are kept alive by money from such sources.

I had possibly my best game for Don Revie's England in the Welsh FA Centenary Match at Wrexham in the next match. Terry Yorath was my immediate opponent and he will probably agree that he had a hard time that night. Terry had the reputation of being a ball-winning type of player, but his ability to hit long, productive balls was often overlooked. He was a better all-round player than he was given credit for and an inspiring captain.

Kevin Keegan was made captain and in an enforced experimental side, Don Revie gave caps to Peter Taylor, the first Third Division player to play for England since Johnny Byrne in 1962, and Phil Boyer. At the time Peter Taylor had strong claims to a regular place in the side. Unfortunately he never fulfilled his promise. He had a good dummy, plenty of speed and crossed well. He was always good fun off the field when he entertained us with his mimicry and Norman Wisdom act. I remember one night in Helsinki when he fell over in a restaurant, Norman Wisdom style, and had us in fits of laughter. Boyer was a good target man in domestic football with sound control and finishing skill, but he lacked the individual skill to make the jump to international football. He was one of a number of excellent First Division players Revie tried whom he must have suspected did not have what it takes. Brian Greenhoff, who was to play so well in Italy, probably came into the same category and so did Tony Towers and Mick Doyle, who came on the trip to North America in 1976. Doyle was a Revie type, a hard competitor who would not admit defeat.

Ray Kennedy, my rival on the left side in midfield, played with me at Wrexham. I was in the middle of the midfield trio and Ray was on the left. Ray is a very quiet, genuine lad, and was very popular with the rest of the players. He is superior to me defensively and also at scoring goals. Nevertheless I think he will agree that his lack of pace has been a weakness in his game.

The trip to America for the US Bicentennial Tournament was a chance to develop some understanding before the World Cup game in Helsinki three weeks later. I played in all three matches enjoying every one of them. We lost 0-1 against Brazil in Los Angeles, and my abiding memory of that match was a sixty-yard pass from the left foot of Roberto Rivelino. It was the sweetest pass I have ever seen. We beat Italy 3-2 in the Yankee Stadium, New York, and as the Italians were in our World Cup group Revie introduced seven newcomers to deny Enzo Bearzot, the Italy manager, the chance of seeing our best players. Revie would do almost anything to gain a tactical advantage. In a match in Switzerland a year earlier he sent the players out in mixed up numbers to try and fool the watching managers of other international sides. Graziani scored twice for Italy in the first half and it looked as though England were going to be over-run but we scored three goals in seven minutes in the second half to surprise even ourselves. Ray Wilkins won praise that day for a fine performance in the centre of midfield. He is a mature lad, very self critical and objective in his assessments, and has the ability to remain an influential member of the side for many years to come. Our final match was a 3-1 victory against Team America, a North American Soccer League side that included Bobby Moore, Tommy Smith and Pele. Because it was not an official US team, that final match did not count as a full international.

The 4-1 victory in Helsinki that followed probably represented the high point in Revie's England career. We had a settled front three in Stuart Pearson, Kevin Keegan and Mike Channon who had played together in three of the last four matches, and the midfield of Francis on the right, Trevor Cherry as anchor man in the middle and me on the left was equally settled, or so it appeared. But by the time the home international season started in September, against Northern Ireland at Wembley, more changes were made. Wilkins replaced the injured Francis and Charlie George came in for the injured Channon in attack. Charlie's career lasted seventy-seven minutes before he was substituted by Gordon Hill. It was one of the saddest things about the England set up in the 1970s that Charlie never made more of his ability. When he was at Arsenal and Derby he was a great player and his first time passes out to the wing were in the 'Budgie' Byrne class. His career was interrupted by a cartilage operation before moving to Southampton, but I think he had ruined it before that. He was a brilliant player who somehow went the wrong way and allowed his image to be tarnished by several incidents. The result of the Ireland match was a disappointing 1-1 draw and it put us in a low state for the trip to Rome the following month for the crucial World Cup game against Italy. Stan Bowles was reinstated to play on the left and we fielded a back four of Dave Clement, the QPR right-back, Emlyn Hughes, Roy McFarland and Mick Mills who had never before played together. Two of the midfield trio were defenders, Trevor Cherry and Brian Greenhoff. We never had a sight of goal. Antognoni scored first for Italy when his free kick hit the oncoming Keegan and deflected past Ray Clemence, and Bettega the second with a diving header.

My immediate opponent was the inappropriately-named Romeo Benetti, the Nobby Stiles-Peter Storey figure of the Italian team. Benetti was not much of a talker. He was more of a starer. He went in hard, occasionally late, but he did not foul me as he fouled Keegan a year later in the return match at Wembley which England won 2-0. That foul on Kevin was a bad one. He went in after Kevin had played the ball and could easily have caused serious injury. Kevin had caught him in the mouth earlier and I think he was waiting for his chance for revenge. However, Benetti is not as outrageous as the other two strongmen in the Italian side, Gentile or Tardelli, and nor is he as devious.

Morale had not improved by the time we were next in action against the Dutch three months later at Wembley. Johan Cruyff dominated the game with the aid of some brilliant players round him. Jan Peters, playing in his second international, netted both goals for Holland and it could easily have been five or six. The Dutch had four men in midfield and Cruyff was often at full-back or wide on the flanks, never where we expected him. Our defenders were pulled into all kinds of positions and confidence drained away completely. It was Trevor Francis's début. What a time to start.

Revie had repeated the mistake of Rome in having two ball-winners in midfield, Greenhoff and Paul Madeley. At half-time he was white faced. 'You've got your pride to play for,' he said. 'You're at Wembley, the home of football, and 90,000 people are out there expecting you to turn it on.' But his attempts to rouse us failed. The match was a disaster. The Dutch concept of total football, of creating space and then filling it with dramatic success, was the opposite of Revie's rigid idea of how to play the game. We were given a painful lesson.

I was one of eight players dropped for the next international, the World Cup game against Luxembourg which England won 5-0. Ray Kennedy took my place on the left in a 4-2-4 formation. I was back against Northern Ireland in Belfast in May when no less than nine new players were brought in. Dennis Tueart headed in a cross from Brian Talbot who came on for Ray Wilkins in the eighty-seventh minute, to give us a 2-1 victory. Three days later came the first of two defeats in the Home Championship, the first time England had ever lost two games in succession at Wembley.

The victory of Wales on the Wednesday was their first ever at Wembley. Peter Shilton fouled Leighton James after Emlyn Hughes slipped up and James scored from the spot. Once again it was an odd selection with both Ray Kennedy and myself in the midfield along with Greenhoff. I was chosen for the match against Scotland on the Saturday but had to drop out with a training injury. Brian Talbot took my place. The Scots won 2-1 and their fans proceeded to dig up the pitch and tear down the goalposts. I was sitting in the stands with some other England reserves. We were surrounded by Scots and regretting that under the new England set up the players were fitted out with easily identifiable blazers.

By the time the England squad was ready to set off to Rio de Janeiro for the start of the South American tour in the summer of 1977, it was obvious from what was being said and written in the press that Don Revie was not going to stay as manager much longer. Les Cocker called us together on the Sunday morning and said he would be in charge at the start of the trip. 'Don has been given a bit of stick and I've told him to have a rest for a few days,' he said. He also said that Revie would be watching Italy's match in Finland (they won 3-0 so virtually clinching the group) and would then fly out to Buenos Aires for England's second match.

Unbeknown to the players and the Football Association International Committee members, Revie had instead gone first to Dubai and agreed a contract to become national manager of the United Arab Emirates for a reputed £100,000 a year. He then went to Helsinki and joined the England squad in Buenos Aires later as he said he would. I do not think the players were too critical about him taking another job. He might well have been sacked anyway, just as Alf Ramsey was three years earlier. But it was the way he did it which incurred people's indignation. The FA did not know about it until they read it in Jeff Powell's article in the *Daily Mail*. The fact that Revie was alleged to have been paid £20,000 for his exclusive revelations only increased the resentment against him.

I felt the FA were justified in taking some kind of action although a ten-year ban for bringing the game into disrepute was too severe. It ended any chance he had of being a manager again in English football. Revie subsequently appealed and had the ban lifted, but the comments by the judge – that he was greedy and deceitful – did more harm to his reputation. It was a sorrowful ending to the career of a man who had been one of the Football League's most successful managers. I have met him on a number of occasions since his resignation and have found him much warmer and more relaxed than when he was England manager.

Ironically, England's results on the South American tour were better than expected, a 0-0 draw in Brazil, a 1-1 draw in Argentina and a 0-0 draw in Uruguay. The only man to suffer pain, besides Revie, was Trevor Cherry, who had two teeth knocked out by Daniel Bertoni and found himself being sent off in Buenos Aires. I did not see the incident. After pulling a muscle in Rio, I was sent home with another injured player, Gordon Hill. Known as 'Merlin the magician', Gordon had had a great spell with Manchester United before a knee problem started to slow him down. He was not particularly popular at

Old Trafford as the other players thought he was too greedy. But he managed to pick up six caps, three by coming on as substitute under Revie, and was one of eighteen forwards used by Revie in his three years as manager.

Revie called up thirteen midfield players, seventeen back-four players and four goalkeepers. In all he used fifty-two players in thirty-one matches. That was far too many. The only player who was almost certain of his place was Ray Clemence, who played in twenty-seven matches. Ron Greenwood, in contrast, has alternated between Clemence and Shilton. The only other regulars under Revie were Kevin Keegan with twenty-four appearances and Mike Channon with twenty-seven.

Within a month of Revie's departure, Greenwood had been appointed England caretaker manager to be in charge for England's last three matches of 1977. As Professor Sir Harold Thompson, the FA chairman said, there was a need to bring some dignity and stability back into English football and Ron was the ideal man to do that. West Ham gave him leave of absence and the players received the news with enthusiasm. As one of his discoveries, I was very pleased about his selection only to learn two weeks later that I was out of the squad for the match against Switzerland!

As a short-term measure to re-establish some understanding, Ron included six Liverpool players in the side plus Kevin Keegan, an ex-Liverpool player, who was at SV Hamburg. The surprise was that Ian Callaghan was included at the age of thirty-five for his first cap since 1966. It seemed a good idea, but it did not work. The Swiss put ten men behind the ball and held on to draw 0-0.

I was back in the squad for the Luxembourg World Cup qualifier a month later, the game England had to win by a lot of goals to put pressure on Italy. I failed to make the side and watched as we struggled to win 2-0. That was the game where we played only three players at the back, Cherry, Watson and Hughes. Trevor Francis, whom Ron had always respected, played up front with Paul Mariner, and Gordon Hill went wide. Paul Mariner took some time to get started but I believe now he is the best all-round striker in England. Not only is he clever on the ground, he's also exceptionally good in the air and it is rare that a striker can combine both these assets.

When England played Italy at Wembley in November we needed a cricket score to qualify for the World Cup finals in Argentina. We knew we could not do it, but our 2-0 victory was very satisfying all the same. I was back in the team. Kevin Keegan was also back after an eight week suspension in West Germany. And Ron Greenwood started the system that was to bring England some success after all the gloom – two forwards, Steve Coppell and Peter Barnes, playing wide on the flanks. Kevin scored the first goal and I got the second, my first for England. Kevin had an outstanding game and I admired his bravery after being continually whacked by Benetti and Tardelli. Kevin is one of the bravest players I have ever seen. He will keep going regardless of the consequences, taking knocks without complaint, and commands the respect of Europe's best defenders. He is immensely powerful for a small man, a result of years of weight training and dedicated running. Some players like weight training but I am not a believer in it. You can become too heavy around the shoulders.

When 'Pop' Robson was at Upton Park he brought his father-in-law, Len Eppel, to talk to the players about balance and movement. Len is an expert dancer and has made a study of movement. He thought I was too lackadaisical in my movements and said this was because I was a casual, relaxed person off the field. He noticed I had a tendency to lounge around on chairs instead of sitting up properly and believed this was an indication of my general attitude. I did not disagree and afterwards tried to concentrate on being sharper. Len said that 'Pop' had been on the slow side earlier in his career but had worked on this weakness and was at that time one of the sharpest players in the game.

Ron Greenwood built up a much happier, more relaxed atmosphere in the England side and it was reflected in our performances. There was less sign of tension. Like Joe Mercer, he told the players to enjoy their football and to express themselves rather than follow a rigid pattern while playing.

However, it was hard to enjoy the next match against West Germany in Munich which we lost 1-2. There had been eight inches of snow on the pitch, yet it played well after the snow had been removed. Stuart Pearson put us ahead and Ronnie Worm, who scored for the West German 'B' team against England 'B' the night before in Augsburg, came on as a substitute and equalized in the seventy-ninth minute. The Germans won the match, rather fortuitously we felt, when Rainer Bonhof scored from a free kick. As Ray Clemence guided the defenders into forming a wall, Mick Mills, the end man, was pulled back by the other players in the wall and Bonhof shot precisely at that moment. The ball brushed Mick's leg and went in. That provoked a forthright inquest afterwards because an international team should not be beaten by a free kick if the wall is far enough over, covering up to a yard beyond the line of the near post. Mick was in the right position originally but was hauled back.

Bonhof is a master at taking free kicks, being almost in the Rivelino class. This is a neglected art in English football. Too often players line up on the far side and a ball is chipped in for someone to try a header. To score a goal from that situation needs a mistake to be made by the defenders and at the highest level few mistakes are made. Ron has always encouraged us to have a shot at goal when the free kick is within shooting range. It is better to attack the goal than not attack it. You can always get a deflection, as Bonhof did. The Continentals and South Americans always seem to have someone in their side who can whip the ball over the wall into the unprotected side of the goal. If the ball is struck at the right pace, it is hard for the goalkeeper to make ground across his goal to stop it. Not many English players can do this. They can bend the ball but not with sufficient pace to be effective. Glenn Hoddle is a notable exception. Glenn concentrates on clipping the ball just over the wall firmly enough to beat the goalkeeper and has scored a high proportion of his goals from free kicks. When he eventually becomes an England regular, this skill will be invaluable.

I was injured when England drew 1-1 with Brazil at Wembley in April which was just as well because the Brazilians earned some critical headlines with their aggressive play. They obstructed opponents wherever possible and had five men cautioned, which is unusual for them and unusual for an international at Wembley.

I have never really had a satisfying Home Championship. In fact, I have missed many games against the home countries. This has not disappointed me too much because playing against players I come across in League matches lacks the appeal of taking on foreign sides. In 1978, I played in the 3-1 defeat of Wales at Cardiff, was injured when we beat Northern Ireland in a drab 1-0 game at Wembley on the Tuesday and came on as substitute at Hampden Park on the Saturday. We finished the Scots game winning 1-0 when goalkeeper Alan Rough dropped a cross from Peter Barnes and Steve Coppell put the ball in the net. Ally MacLeod, trying to whip his team into the right mental state for the World Cup that summer, caused some mirth in the England camp when he said: 'I just cannot accept losing today. We were tremendous and England were terrible. What made it worse was that the goal was scored by the worst player on the park!' I don't think he watched the same match!

England ended the 1977-78 international season with a convincing 4-1 win over Hungary at Wembley. Hungary were on their way to Argentina, along with Scotland, and we had beaten both of them. While the Scots went on their unhappy trip to South America, we were getting ready for the European Championship the following season. The opening game was in Copenhagen in September 1978 and we gave Ron Greenwood a nightmare by scraping through 4-3. 'I'm an advocate of attacking football, but this carried it to extremes,' he said afterwards. The 1-1 draw in Dublin against Ireland a month later proved our hardest match, as we had feared. With players of the calibre of Frank Stapleton, David O'Leary, Liam Brady and Gerry Daly, Ireland were rated the biggest danger in our group and justifiably so. Stapleton rivals Mariner in his all-round skills. He works hard, has good awareness of situations and finishes well with head and feet. For a tall, gangly man, O'Leary is physically very strong. You rarely see him knocked off the ball. His speed, added to his defensive qualities, have made him one of the outstanding defenders in Europe.

Injury kept me out of the 1-0 victory on a frozen pitch against the Czechs in November 1978 but I played in the 4-0 victory over Northern Ireland the following February. Bob Latchford scored twice, but it was Keegan's game – he was brilliant. Perhaps our best performance in 1979 came in Sofia when we beat Bulgaria 3-0 to all but clinch our place in Rome for the finals. On that trip we drew 0-0 in Sweden, a poor game, and lost 4-3 to Austria in Vienna, a virtual repeat of the Denmark match. Ray Wilkins and I were over-run in midfield in the first half and we went 3-1 down before recovering, too late, in the second half.

England beat Denmark and Bulgaria, as expected, at home, and Northern Ireland away, and so came top of the group with fifteen points from eight matches, seven points ahead of Northern Ireland. The inquests about what went wrong in Italy in the finals were long and painful, and still no satisfactory, all-embracing answer has come up. In retrospect, I feel it did not help to have taken part in a Home Championship three weeks before we left for Italy without the overseas players, Keegan, Woodcock and Cunningham and also Nottingham Forest's Peter Shilton and Viv Anderson, who were playing in the European Cup Final. I am pleased to see that the FA have changed the format of the Home Championship. Having it all at the end of the season when players are tired or have their minds on more important championships does not work.

We had a disastrous Home Championship, losing 1-4 to Wales at Wrexham, drawing with Northern Ireland in front of an apathetic Wembley crowd in midweek and marginally relieving the gloom by beating Scotland 2-0 at Hampden Park with me scoring one of the goals. The confidence gained from England's best two results in the Rome build up – the 2-0 win in Spain and the 3-1 victory over world champions Argentina at Wembley – had been largely lost. We were also without Trevor Francis whose Achilles tendon injury had cruelly interrupted his long-anticipated emergence as a striker of true international class.

We were on edge before the opening game of the European Championships against the unrated Belgians in Turin, and it showed in our play. The Belgians kept catching us offside which should not have happened so frequently. Ray Wilkins chipped a fine goal and Ceulemans equalized to make the final score 1-1. A controversial offside decision stopped Tony

Woodcock scoring and as Ron Greenwood said afterwards, that decision was probably the difference between success and failure. As the Italians drew 0-0 with Spain the same day in Milan, dropping a point did not matter so much. We just had to get a good result against Italy in Turin three days later.

Ron called me in for a private talk before that game and explained that he was putting Ray Kennedy in my place. With the Italians marking the front men man-to-man he wanted a more defensive player on the left to hold that side while Kenny Sansom went forward and tried to get behind the defence. David Johnson was dropped and Garry Birtles, a late replacement in the squad, was picked to play up front with his former Nottingham Forest team mate Tony Woodcock. Birtles had shown his ability to take on a man-to-man marker in the European Cup Final and Ron Greenwood was clearly looking for a repeat performance.

Kevin Keegan was in midfield, where he had been for some time, but in my view his best position is still probably up front because he shields the ball so well and is so brave and hard working. The greatest performance of his career was when he was playing for Liverpool against Borussia Moenchengladbach in the European Cup Final in May 1977. His domination of that fine defender Bertie Vogts was the finest display I have ever seen from an England player breaking up a defence.

The match against Italy did not go well for us and was dominated by the defences. Mariner came on as substitute in the second half for the tiring Birtles, but it was too late to alter the course of the game. We were defeated 0-1 when Tardelli scored from Graziani's cross after Phil Neal over-committed himself. The nearest we came to scoring was when Ray Kennedy struck the post.

We were out of the finals and the 2-1 victory against Spain in Naples three days later with a much-changed side that included me was no consolation. Not even one of my rare goals could make up for the acute disappointment. Perhaps the press had built us up too much on the strength of the Spain and Argentina wins earlier. But those matches were friendlies. In real competition we had failed.

For the first time in his England job, Ron Greenwood found

himself being criticized and he particularly resented attacks on him made by the ITV panel. His selection of Birtles had been questioned. The inquests droned on. But in football you have little time to dwell on the past. There is always another competition looming. For us, it was the qualifying group of the World Cup which saw us matched with Norway, Romania, Switzerland and Hungary. The 4-0 beating of Norway at Wembley drew some criticism but I thought it was a good result. I missed the 1-2 defeat in Romania because of a groin strain. Our 2-1 success over Switzerland in November was also greeted sceptically. It was a two-tone performance. In the first half we were brilliant, while in the second we faded alarmingly, upsetting Greenwood, who reminded us that people always remember the last part of a match and tend to forget what has gone before.

In April a disappointing goalless draw with Romania at Wembley left us with five points from four games. Hungary began their group matches in fine style and so our two away fixtures at the end of the season, against Switzerland and Hungary, became increasingly significant.

The mood of a tour is always set by the first result and when we lost 1-2 in Basle it meant the rest of the week was depressing. As in the Brazil, Wales and Scotland games, I was not even on the bench and I was wondering whether my international career was over. Some people suggested that I was tired after a long season; I had played more than fifty matches but I wasn't tired. I had had an indifferent spell around the time of the League Cup final but all players have a bad trot at some time. I wanted to play for England again because I knew I could still do it.

I suspected the atmosphere in the dressing room would be very low after the Switzerland defeat so I didn't go in. I had already asked Ron Greenwood for permission to go into town for a meal with Hilkka who was over for 3 days. I could imagine how the players were feeling: they had done reasonably well in the first twenty-five minutes and had then conceded two really bad goals. Some of England's 'fans' had misbehaved and suddenly it was Turin all over again – not that the fighting on the terraces was any excuse. In the few days after the match the players were ringing home and hearing the press reports so it was an unhappy party of players, officials and journalists that arrived in Budapest for the match against Hungary.

A point that I felt had been overlooked on the Basle game was that Ron Greenwood had only had his full-strength team together the day before the match when the Liverpool players arrived after the European Cup final. Twenty-four hours is not long enough to prepare a team for a vital World Cup game. But there was a whole week to prepare for the Hungary match and it enabled us to be more settled.

There was no indication during training what team would be selected. Usually players can guess what is happening by the way training goes: if a certain back four is used in training sessions it is probable that they will play in the match. But this time there were no clues. The team was supposed to be announced on the Thursday after training but Ron delayed it until the Friday. He said there was no reflection on the younger players who had not had the best of luck in previous games but this time he was going to play experienced men whose last chance it was to make the World Cup finals. I was relieved to hear I was included and I felt ready for the game after nearly a month off.

The grim mood of the four slowly changed as the jokes came pouring out about Dad's Army. 'You'll need some practice getting your boots on,' said Kevin Keegan. 'You've been in cobwebs that long!' Whenever I approached the lads broke into the Dad's Army signature tune.

We arrived at the Nep Stadium ninety minutes before the kick-off and it was already full with 68,000 fans creating a tremendous noise after seeing Ferenc Puskas, visiting his homeland for the first time since 1965, score a hat-trick in a warm-up game. The pitch was the best playing surface I have ever stepped out on and I was also pleased to see that it was a big pitch. The bigger the pitch, the less chance of one of those tight negative games that I dislike so much. We knew we had to win, but there was less pressure than you would expect. No-one thought we would win.

We had been warned that the Hungarians would come storming at us in the opening half-hour and when they didn't we took the initiative ourselves and took the game to them. In the eighteenth minute Terry McDermott went towards the by-line on the right and I sensed that he was going to pull the ball back first time towards me. The ball clipped someone on the way and was spinning as it came to me.

My hit was not clean, in the sense that I caught it on the instep, but it wasn't quite the miss-hit some people claimed. It caught my toe but went where I had intended, towards the near post where the goalkeeper was unsighted. For a split second it looked as though it might go outside the post but it curled back in and I was never more pleased to score a goal. Perhaps if I had met the ball sweetly it would have gone straight to the keeper. My intention was to make sure it was on target and it was.

Just before half-time I felt a slight strain in the groin and during the interval Ray Wilkins warmed up in case he had to replace me. I said to Ron: 'Give me five minutes and see how it goes.' Seconds before the interval Garaba equalised for Hungary but that was less of a blow than the millions of television viewers at home thought because there was so little time left for the Hungarians to capitalise on it. If there had been ten minutes left they might have made it awkward for us. As it was we were able to come out in the second half and play just as well as we had done in the first.

My second goal in the sixtieth minute was the finest shot I have ever struck. Phil Neal passed to Kevin on the right side of the box and Kevin laid it back into my path as I ran into the box. I hit it first time with my left foot and as I looked up I saw the ball was on target for the angle of post and bar. There was just one reservation in my mind. Continental balls tend to swerve and I feared that might happen this time as there was a long way to go before it reached the goal. Fortunately the ball never deviated an inch. It went straight into the stanchion and stuck there. 'That's an unbelievable goal for you,' said Kevin.

At home Hilkka, who was watching with my parents, said: 'I had to look twice at the screen to make sure it was Trevor.' I have never powered in a goal like that in my career. It was my eleventh wedding anniversary and what a way to celebrate! Soon afterwards, I was caught in a late tackle on the ankle and it aggravated my groin. I signalled to the bench that Ray should come on and I went off right after Kevin scored England's third goal from the penalty spot. It was a somewhat dubious penalty – one you expect for the home side, not the away side.

As the final whistle sounded the television men grabbed Kevin and me for an interview before the lines went and we were late getting back into the dressing room to savour the excitement of having retrieved our World Cup chances. Ron wasn't too happy about that, he said the television hadn't been given permission. But it all seemed incidental in the joy of the moment. We were back in with a chance of qualifying for Spain. It couldn't have been a better ending to the tour, or for me to a memorable season.

In the restaurant that night the other players broke into their version of 'I'm Forever Blowing Bubbles' as we celebrated an historic victory. And on the plane home the next day, the pilot announced: 'We are travelling at 550 miles an hour – slower than Trevor's second but faster than his first!'

A week after the Budapest game it was announced that I was being awarded the MBE in the Queen's Birthday Honours List. I was very thrilled about the news. What a week it had been – two goals in the Nep Stadium, my wedding anniversary, Hilkka's birthday and an honour from the Queen!

11

Are we too Insular?

English football has been accused of being too insular and inward looking and the critics have a case that needs answering. We tend to persist in saying that our League is the best in the world while we have failed to qualify for successive World Cup finals in 1974 and 1978. The English Football League is the most competitive and probably has the greatest strength in depth, but the way in which it is organized does not encourage the development of outstanding ball players.

Right from early days at school, our footballers are asked to work, chase and harry, and this carries through to the top level. It makes for a spectacle and the crowds like it, but I do not think it is a coincidence that the greatest player produced in the British Isles in recent years was from Northern Ireland, George Best, and the other footballing hero of recent times, Kevin Keegan, had to go to West Germany before his full talents were realized. Our system tends to produce good hard-working competitive players, not great ones.

The way England ignored the Gold Cup tournament in Uruguay at the start of 1981 was said by some people to typify our attitude to world football. It was a commemorative competition to celebrate the fiftieth anniversary of the first World Cup in 1930, and all the previous winners were invited. Only England declined to attend and the way the Brazilians, Uruguayans and Argentinians dominated the event with an array of promising newcomers showed that our absence could prove a mistake. The FA tried to ensure that a squad of players was chosen from a restricted number of clubs so as not to interfere with the League programme, and eventually had to conceed that it could not be done. The League programme had to be given priority, once again, over the needs of the national side. In most other countries the national side comes first.

When England won the World Cup in 1966 it lifted the whole nation and our sporting prestige stood at its highest level for years. We had a good side, a good system and some quality players. Many of those players were still in the squad when we went to Mexico to defend our title in 1970. George Cohen and Ray Wilson had gone, replaced by Keith Newton and Terry Cooper. Alan Mullery was in to do the Nobby Stiles job and at centre-half Everton's Brian Labone had taken over from Jack Charlton. Moore, Hurst and Peters were still there and so was Bobby Charlton.

A mistake by Jeff Astle when he came on as a second-half substitute against Brazil may well have been the difference between England retaining the World Cup and ultimate failure. Astle's miss left Brazil 1-0 winners against England and winners of Group C. Pele and his fellow Brazilians had to admit there was nothing between the two teams. Yet while England lost that self-defeating quarter-final to the West Germans, Brazil went on to outplay the Italians 4-1 in the final. If Astle had not missed against Brazil, if Gordon Banks had not been ill for the West Germany match, England, not Brazil, might have won the tournament. England's midfield quartet of Ball, Mullery, Charlton and Peters was probably as fine a midfield as we have ever fielded. It had skill, experience and balance and up front the strength and finishing power of Geoff Hurst was complemented by the opportunism and bravery of Francis Lee.

Before the 1974 World Cup, Charlton had gone and so had Hurst. Charlton was irreplaceable. No one could quite do what he did or have the same influence. Martin Chivers, Joe Royle, Malcolm Macdonald, Peter Osgood, Frank Worthington, Mike Channon and David Johnson were replacements for Hurst and only Chivers up to 1974 had a reasonably long run in the striker position. The problem then, as now, was that there were a lot of very good players to pick from and few great ones whose ability demanded a place.

Colin Bell came into midfield, but his career was prematurely ended by injury. And Roy McFarland, the Derby centre-half, was also troubled by persistent injury. I consider McFarland's injury to have been a key factor in England's decline during the mid-seventies. Fully fit, he was one of the world's leading defenders.

Of increasing significance for the national side over this barren period was that more and more good players, including Bell, McFarland and Kevin Beattie were suffering with bad injuries. More recently Trevor Francis and Ray Wilkins have been out of the game for extended periods. It would be interesting to have some statistics of how the incidence of injury among leading English players compares with the incidence of injury among top players in Europe and South America. I believe a greater number of players are injured in the Football League because it is more physically demanding and the pressure of matches on players is greater.

In many countries it is possible for the best players to take part in domestic matches which they know they will win because of the gulf in class among the various teams. Here, the talent is so widely spread that a First Division team can never take success for granted in any match. Players have to apply themselves to the maximum in every game and that, plus the fact that we tend to play roughly a third more matches in a season, leads to wear-and-tear injuries such as a pelvic strain. Ray Wilkins is the latest of an increasing number of players who has needed an operation after this most depressing of injuries. A pelvic strain often needs six months rest before a player can start training properly, and only a broken leg takes longer.

Many well known players have had trouble in the pelvic region, among them Frank Lampard and Billy Bonds of West Ham, Peter Taylor, now with Orient, Don McAllister of Spurs, Steve Williams of Southampton and even Alan Mullery when he was still playing. English players play on a variety of pitches ranging from extremely muddy to hard and frosty surfaces and I believe this is upsetting to certain types of muscles in the body. The extra strain that is imposed during our long almost unending season leads to weaknesses and eventually something snaps as it did with Trevor Francis.

Trevor's Achilles tendon break when he was just running was probably the most tragic of all the wear-and-tear injuries which have affected some of England's best players. He had just shown world-class form during England's victory in Spain and we were pinning our hopes of success in the European Championship in Rome on his partnership with Tony Woodcock. He had convinced everyone he was the type of player England needed, extremely fast and a brilliant finisher. To the relief of Ron Greenwood and his coaches, when Trevor returned to the Nottingham Forest side he showed he was as good as ever and his serious injury had not affected his pace in any way.

Arsenal captain David O'Leary was another player to be out for a long spell with Achilles tendon trouble. His tendon did not snap as Trevor's had done, but a strain caused him to miss sixteen matches in the first half of the 1980-81 season.

A great number of players in recent seasons have been afflicted by hamstring strains, including myself, and perhaps the most notable of them was Kevin Keegan. The danger with this particular type of injury is that it starts to feel as though it has cleared up and the player returns to action only to find that the muscle goes again. This happened to Kevin. I have had a number of hamstring strains myself. They are dreaded by most players.

I remember Kevin telling me that he usually played around forty league and cup matches in the West German Bundesliga. Brian Talbot of Arsenal played sixty-nine matches in the 1979-80 season. If England are to build a winning side at the highest competitive level in world football again our international players should play fewer matches. They must be given more time to prepare as the leading European and South American countries prepare. It is not fair that our internationals should be expected to play a hard League match on a Saturday and go out to face world-class opponents in a World Cup game the following Wednesday. Some critics will say that when Don Revie managed to persuade the Football League to postpone matches the Saturday before an international the idea was a failure. I do not accept that. Revie failed because he tried to impose too rigid a system on an England side which did not have the day to day involvement that he had at Leeds and was necessary to create the teamwork for it to be successful.

The First Division should be reduced from twenty-two to eighteen clubs, cutting the number of League games from forty-two to thirty-four in a season. This would give the League scope to allow the England manager to work with his squad. I appreciate that the four unlucky clubs who will have to drop to the Second Division will object strongly. Their loss of revenue will be immense, but I consider the welfare of English football as a whole to be more important than the welfare of four clubs.

While standards have improved abroad, ours have declined. There are few players in England with the technical ability to control the ball and who are prepared to take on opponents in areas of the field where there is a risk that a mistake could be punished by a goal. The average English defender sees his job as to defend, and put in a situation where he gains possession near his penalty area, he will kick the ball away to safety. Coaches will encourage him to do this. It relieves the pressure on the defence for a few seconds and the midfield and attackers can fight for the ball in the safe end of the pitch.

This negative attitude comes from the fear of losing. It comes from a manager who knows that unless he produces results he will be sacked. It comes from crowds who want only victories, not defeats. The lack of defenders who can attack is now one of the basic weaknesses in the English game. The kind of player we need is the Paul Breitner type when he was in his prime in the West German side. He was an extra forward when the Germans had the ball. The Dutch also had players of this type in Rudi Krol and Wim Suurbier, and the Brazilians had Carlos Alberto.

George Cohen was an attacking full-back for England and so was Terry Cooper. Both were capable of going forward and getting crosses in. They were substitute wingers. I believe that Kenny Sansom is in the same mould. Because there are so few genuine wingers around, full-back play has withered and now there are not so many good full-backs left either. I thought the Leeds experiment of playing a former winger Eddie Gray at full-back was an interesting development that could be followed by other clubs. Eddie has the skill to do the kind of job I am talking about.

In West Germany the *libero*, or sweeper, is a key player

because he is the one man who is not marked man-to-man and has the licence to go forward into attack. Invariably the best player is moved to that position, first Franz Beckenbauer and now it is Bernd Schuster, the twenty-two-year-old who was the star of the 1980 European Championship. The English fear of losing is one reason why the *libero* idea is not tried here. We still use the zonal system with four players at the back. If a player is beaten, there is always someone to cover. The midfield players will be encouraged to get back behind the ball. Ron Greenwood has tried to introduce the sweeper into the England side with his successful use of Bryan Robson of West Bromwich Albion in the role, and Malcolm Allison, in his second spell at Crystal Palace, tried a similar experiment using Gerry Francis as a sweeper. However, I cannot see it catching on at club level.

Abroad, national prestige comes from success at international level. Here we still tend to look at our game through the eyes of the clubs. When it is time for our outstanding players to go into action in international football they have already had a physically-draining nine- or ten-month period of non-stop competitive football and are jaded. At the end of the season most of the players are looking forward to a rest, not the Home Championship and then a European tour and World Cup or European Championship matches.

If it was not for the income from gate receipts which keeps alive the Welsh, Scottish and Northern Ireland Football Associations, the Home Championship could well be scrapped. It raises no enthusiasm among the players and little excitement among supporters, except the Scots whose wild forays into England led to them being refused tickets for the 1981 match. In its present form it is a competition that we could all do without, except for the opportunities it may give for team managers to try out new young hopefuls.

The frantic pace of English League football has led to a decline in the number of players with creative flair, and individual skill has tended to disappear from many sides. The skilful player has not been encouraged by managers and coaches. Players like Frank Worthington, Stan Bowles, Alan Hudson and Tony Currie are viewed with suspicion. They are termed 'luxury' players because they seemingly do not contribute so much to the team effort as other players.

Fortunately I have been immune to this at West Ham. Both Ron Greenwood and John Lyall have allowed me to play in an attacking manner and have not restricted me to defensive duties which are not my strength. This would not be the case at many other clubs. It was interesting to read the comment made by Cesar Menotti, manager of the Argentine side, when Osvaldo Ardiles returned to play for his country in the Gold Cup tournament after playing in the English League. Menotti said that Ardiles had picked up some bad habits in England such as chasing back to defend and playing too many square balls. 'I want him to attack and play positive balls,' said Menotti.

As so many players in a normal English League game are told to get back behind the ball when a move breaks down, it is extremely difficult, even for a player of the class of Ardiles, to play many telling, forward passes. I am constantly in this position myself. Looking up to see a mass of bodies in front of you the only option left is to play the ball square. In England the policy is to deny the opposing midfield players time and space. On the Continent and in South America, the tendency is to let the other side attack and then try to regain possession just outside the box to launch a counter attack. Foreign coaches and managers are more prepared to gamble. They are saying 'See what you can do with the ball and when we get it, we will see what we can do.' Players on one side will match their ability on the ball against the ball skill of their opponents. There is far less hustling and harrying and not so many tackles. It is a more open type of football, more skilled and with a greater element of risk. I am not sure English audiences would like it. They have been brought up on whole-hearted commitment and enthusiasm and it is hard to change the watching habits of a lifetime. Skill is appreciated here but not as much as it should be. I can understand a player like Raimondo Ponte, the Swiss international, coming here and wondering what he has let himself in for by joining Nottingham Forest. Our system is much different to the system he has been used to in Europe.

The Yugoslav players have adapted better to our way of playing because their League is more like ours and possession of the ball is disputed the way it is here. The arrival of Arnold

Muhren and Frans Thijssen at Ipswich has provided the one instance where foreign players have significantly influenced the pattern of play of their new club and I believe it is one of the reasons why Ipswich have become challengers to Liverpool for the title of Britain's outstanding club side.

When Muhren and Thijssen first played together at Portman Road they found the ball being played over their heads to the front players. That was the Ipswich style from the days of Sir Alf Ramsey – get the ball up to the strikers as quickly as possible for them to knock it down for the oncoming midfield players. To his credit, Bobby Robson, the Ipswich manager, realized that he was not getting the best value from his two Dutchmen and asked his players to adopt a more patient approach by playing shorter balls into midfield from the back. Thijssen, the more rugged of the two, plays wide on the right and prefers to run on the ball and beat opponents, while Muhren, playing wide on the left, is the long-range passer, usually with his left foot. Thijssen soon proved himself to be the best foreign acquisition in English football with Muhren not far behind.

A favourite phrase of many English managers when interviewed after matches is 'I thought the lads battled superbly'. They are referring to the competitive instincts of the players and the way they kept going at maximum throttle for the whole ninety minutes. Most clubs seek to be consistent and they are more likely to get good results if they compete. To play badly but still get a result is the compromise many managers look for from their team. They realize that no side can play to its full capability in every match. Often it seems this competitive quality is savoured more than pure skill. The ideal, of course, is to compete and have skill and West Ham have striven to achieve that balance with, I believe, considerable success. When we go a goal behind, we do not lose heart as we may have been accused of doing in the past. There were many games in the 1979-80 season when we went behind and came back to win. It became one of the hallmarks of the side.

Frans Thijssen and Arnold Muhren would be much less effective if they were playing in the Second Division. As most players in the Division are less skilled, the games are more physical and rarely flow. The action is largely confined to long balls dropped into each penalty area which as a consequence becomes a battleground. An accurately struck long pass can be one of the most damaging passes in a player's repertoire, but too often in English football the long ball is played when there is no chance of it being used profitably. It is played as an easy means of quickly transferring play from one end of the pitch to the other and putting pressure on defenders and until we start producing defenders with more all round skill, I cannot see this changing.

I mentioned earlier the importance of the pass because it enables a team to retain possession. The Continentals seem much more reluctant than us to relinquish this possession. A classic example of possession football was the display Brazil gave at Wembley in May 1981. They delighted everyone with their control, back heels and flicks, but more than anything they rarely gave the ball away with a slack pass. I am sure that the missing ingredient in our game today is one of individual skill and flair.

The skill deficiencies among our players can be traced back to their formative years. The time to pick up good habits such as kicking the ball properly, controlling it and passing it, are learned roughly from the age of six upwards. By the time youngsters are allowed to train with professional clubs at the age of thirteen it is usually too late to eradicate the bad habits they have picked up earlier. Too many children under twelve are pushed into competitive football before they master the basics, and the reason why our players are so aggressive and hard to beat can be seen at most grounds all over the country where school and youth matches take place. The teachers and fathers of the boys will be standing on the touchline urging their offspring to get stuck in. Systems like 4-3-3 and 4-4-2 are used and boys are brought up to think that football is about keeping one's position, marking an opponent and making sure he does not pass you. The positive things, such as getting the ball forward, finding space, going on runs with the ball, beating opponents and using both the inside and outside of both feet are overlooked in the rush and bustle. The skilful youngster is not given much chance to improve his skills.

Throughout my career I have, at different times, been

involved with schoolboy coaching. I am sure coaches, teachers and even dads must concentrate more on convincing youngsters that to become a professional footballer their first priority is to learn the basic arts of how to kick, head and control a ball. A number of times I have taken a squad of boys and after a little while one will ask: 'When are we going to have a game, sir?' The sad fact is that if they were put into a game it would emphasize that they did not possess the necessary ability to create a flowing match. That is only achieved through hours and hours of practice.

The lack of adequate facilities and equipment because of cost is another drawback. I have become associated in a coaching capacity with the Eurosports Village near Ipswich. It was originally a Naval base called HMS Ganges which has now been converted into an extensive sports complex. My involvement centres mainly around the numerous schoolboy football clinics that are run throughout the year. They also cater for the non-league or foreign amateur side who might want to spend a week or more of intensive training. There are endless outdoor and indoor facilities available and it's encouraging to see such developments taking place in sport. Hopefully, on the course I attend there, I can make sure that the players are principally involved in improving their skill.

Skill comes from spending hours kicking a ball against a wall or fence and controlling the return, as I did when I was a boy. Glenn Hoddle, likewise, used to perform a similar exercise in his garden and that may explain why he is one of the most skilful players in our game. In addition to his two-footed skills, Glenn has shooting ability in the Bobby Charlton class and has become the highest-scoring English-born midfield player in present day football. When he made his senior début against Bulgaria in 1979 he scored a spectacular goal from the edge of the box and appeared to be certain of a regular place in the side. However, a couple of disappointing under-21 matches followed and it took him some time to establish himself at senior level.

Despite his skill and finesse, Glenn is still being criticized for not putting enough into his game. He does not win enough tackles, it is said. He is looked on as a luxury player, as Bowles, Worthington, Currie and Hudson were in their differing styles.

He is more like a Continental player than an English player and I think his future eventually could well lie abroad where he would be more appreciated.

At professional level, in their efforts to produce a winning side, many managers and coaches are concentrating too much on making players all-rounders instead of helping them improve the parts of their game in which they excel. I think this is a mistaken attitude. It does not happen in other sports. The England cricket selectors do not ask Geoff Boycott to brush up his bowling because they want him to open both bowling and batting. They let him spend all his time improving what he is good at – batting. In America, the baseball pitchers are not told they have to be good batters as well. The quarterback in American football is not asked to carry out a multitude of roles. At the highest levels, a player should be allowed to specialize and his contribution should be balanced by the contributions of players with different skills. A football team needs a mixture of good defenders who can mark and tackle, midfield players who can pass and create openings and finishers who can score goals. Until we change our system one player cannot be expected to be a complete all-round player capable of filling every role.

I was amazed recently when I discovered that Alan Hudson had played only twice for England, against Cyprus and West Germany, when we won both matches, scoring an aggregate total of seven goals to nil. He had tremendous skill and should have earned many more caps but he lacked dedication and did not prepare himself as he should have done. Don Revie left him out for this reason not because he doubted his ability. Hudson later went to North America and was a star with Seattle Sounders. His manager, Alan Hinton, later described him as the best trainer he had ever worked with.

Malcolm Macdonald scored all five goals against Cyprus but did not have the all-round ability needed to hold down the position of England striker. He excelled as a finisher, but a player needs more than finishing ability to succeed in international matches. If Revie had been able to call upon a combination of Macdonald and Mike Channon he would have had a very fine player. Mike was outstanding as an individual player, but his finishing let him down.

Currie, who played only seventeen times for England, should also have gained more caps. He had exceptional ability and his use of the long ball was not bettered by any of his rivals for an England place. Unfortunately, injuries stopped him when he was in his prime.

Southampton's Steve Williams is a contender for a place in the present England side. He is a sound, all-round player and very competitive, but he has yet to show that he has the extra qualities needed for the highest level. The same could apply to Gordon Cowans, Villa's inside-forward. Alan Devonshire, my West Ham colleague, is among the latest crop of players who I think could make the breakthrough into the senior side. He has the two vital qualities – pace and the ability to beat opponents – as well as skill and could play wide on the left. Ron Greenwood likes players of his style who can play on the flank.

There is no short answer to the problem of lack of skill in English football. Our approach at school level needs to be drastically changed and there should be more emphasis on ball work and fewer competitive matches. Five-a-side matches under the age of twelve could replace full-sized matches. As for boys practising themselves as I did there is less likelihood of that happening now than in my youth because the modern boy has so many distractions – television, video recorders, tape recorders, TV games and records among them. As families have become more affluent, so the chances of a youngster going out with a ball and kicking it against a wall have diminished. The most skilful young players will continue to come from Brazil, Argentina, Uruguay and the less-developed countries where success at football is a means of escaping from poverty. But if our youngsters can be steered in the right direction and encouraged to work hard enough, we should be able to improve the skill factor in our game.

12

Money

It is not necessary to be an accountant to realize that something is drastically wrong with the finances of football. When a club is prepared to pay out £1 million, the equivalent of its total income through the gate for a whole year, on buying a player whose career could be finished in one tackle, then certain people in the game are taking unjustified risks. The upward spiral of transfer fees has resulted from too much money chasing too few players. This has been bad for the game. Most of the money for these deals is borrowed so that repayments and crippling interest charges produce intolerable burdens on club finances. The future of even the biggest of clubs is jeopardized. When Liverpool, the most successful club in the land, have to start making staff economies then the situation really is worrying.

If it is foolhardy to pay out inflationary transfer fees, why do clubs do it? Firstly, managers believe that one more good player could just make the difference and transform their side into a championship team and take it into Europe with all the added revenue that follows. That rarely happens, although it must be conceded that Brian Clough's £1 million purchase of Trevor Francis helped Nottingham Forest retain the European Cup. Secondly, there is a shortage of talent within the Football League. People are always saying 'there aren't the players about there used to be in my day', and it is true at the moment that overall standards have dropped. Because the game is about scoring goals, the players chiefly in demand are always strikers and the fact that Norwich chairman Sir Arthur South talked about asking £2 million for Justin Fashanu, an inexperienced player with less than two years experience of first-team football, is an indication of the distortion of values brought about by a falling off in supply. In my view this is a ridiculous amount. If Fashanu is worth that, how much would Geoff Hurst have been worth on today's scale?

The two transfers which are usually cited to convey the idiocy of the present transfer market are Malcolm Allison's purchases of Steve Daley from Wolves for £1.4 million and Michael Robinson from Preston for £750,000 when he was Manchester City's manager. During the time Daley was at Wolves I always thought he looked a fair player, but to elevate him to superstar status was grossly unfair to him. The Manchester City fans were expecting a world beater for that money and the pressure on Daley was too much. He had to be released to America for a vastly reduced sum. Robinson's move from Preston was probably more disturbing because subsequently every time a manager was asked if his striker was available the first sum he thought of was £750,000 – the fee paid to Preston for an inexperienced player. It became the going rate even for some average players.

In the two years from 5 January 1979, Manchester City's turnover in the transfer market was a colossal £9,036,277, as forty players came and went at Maine Road. The sum paid out was £5,226,277 and the money received £3,810,000. However, apart from the deficit of £1,416,277 on their dealings, City still owed money on transactions spread over a number of years. For example, repayment of the £1,250,000 fee for Kevin Reeves, who transferred from Norwich in 1980, was spread out over four years. Half-way through the 1980-81 season, apparently, Norwich were still owed half their money.

To stop this long-term indebtedness, I would advocate that all transfer fees should be paid during the season when the transfer took place. If a player is bought in January, the whole amount of the fee would have to be paid off by April which would immediately reduce transfer fees. I was disappointed that the Football League chairman rejected a proposal that all transfers should be paid within a year with half the money being laid out at the start. Some restriction is necessary to force clubs to conduct their financial affairs more realistically. This proposal failed to get the necessary threequarters majority, which is itself an artificial limit in my view. If a simple majority is enough to pass Government policies in Parliament, then this system should also apply in football. Instead of money being paid out in exorbitant fees, particularly to foreign clubs, the savings from reduced fees could be used to improve ground facilities. The standards at many grounds are well below what they should be and need to be improved if we are to attract the family audience back to the game. The Football League should also impose a ceiling on transfer fees. Abroad, there is a scale laid down by UEFA which is related to the players' wages and that seems to work. Transfer fees are much lower than in England, but players' wages are much higher. It should be possible for the League to agree on an upper limit and I suggest £500,000 would be ample.

I realize that West Ham may be accused of contributing to the rampant inflation within the game by paying £565,000 for Phil Parkes and £800,000 for Paul Goddard, but in each case the money came from income and the club did not have to go heavily into debt to fund the transfers. Goddard's fee was largely paid for by the money received during our FA Cup success in 1979-80 and our League Cup run. He was a good buy because he supplied something that was missing in the side – a quick-turning, skilful type of player who could complement David Cross.

Clive Allen scored more goals than Paul when they were together at QPR but I have always looked on Paul as the better all-round player. Allen is a great finisher and his scoring record while at Rangers was impressive, but he was less successful in the First Division. That does not mean he lacks the ability to make the grade in the First Division. In his first season there his rapid shuttling from club to club was so bewildering that he did not have a fair chance to prove his worth. I felt very sorry for him. His £1 million move from QPR to Arsenal and then on to Crystal Palace in a £1 million exchange for Kenny Sansom must have puzzled many people. With two million people unemployed and the country in the middle of one of its worst recessions, here was a footballer aged nineteen supposedly making more out of his £1 million transfers than the average fitter at British Leyland makes in a lifetime's work. Of course it was not really like that as Terry Venables, the then Palace manager said at the time, but the impression remains with the public that football is living in a world apart. The five per cent cut of the fee which a player was entitled to make from a transfer has now been abolished, but there is still a lot of money to be made from a mutually agreed signing-on fee.

Tottenham Hotspur were another club which spent a lot of money on strikers – £800,000 for Steve Archibald from Aberdeen and £600,000 for Garth Crooks from Stoke in 1980. The previous season Osvaldo Ardiles and Glenn Hoddle were creating a lot of chances, but many of them were being squandered. Hoddle, a midfield player, finished the season the club's leading scorer. The expenditure of £1.4 million may have seemed a good investment particularly as Archibald and Crooks soon started scoring goals, but coming on top of the club's £3 million redevelopment of their main stand, it was a huge outlay for a club even with Tottenham's resources.

The trouble with £1 million plus fees is that they restrict the number of clubs that can enter the bidding. Even successful clubs such as Ipswich would not be able to afford £1 millon for a player. Bobby Robson's highest outlay in his twelve years at Portman Road has been a mere £200,000. As Ipswich do not own their own ground and cannot use it as security for a bank loan, they have to meet their debts largely out of income. They cannot afford to go heavily into debt. That could be an example for other clubs to follow.

The rapidly-rising transfer fees have unsettled the structure of players' wages. No player is going to move in a £1 million deal unless he is going to be paid a substantial increase in wages. So by agreeing to high transfer fees, club directors have put more pressure on themselves by having to pay higher wages all round. It is now a common complaint in board rooms that players are being greedy. But the impetus for this spiralling wage structure was provided by the clubs themselves when they allowed transfer fees to get out of hand. It is inevitable that the loyal player who has been at the same club all his life is going to say: 'If this new fellow is on £X a week, then I should get an increase as well.'

When Ted MacDougall was signed by West Ham from

Manchester United for a then club record fee of £170,000 in 1973, Ron Greenwood called a meeting of the first-team squad at Upton Park and said that Ted had accepted a wage cut for the remaining three months of the season so his wages would not be out of line with ours. He also said our wages would be upgraded at the end of the season accordingly. That told us our wage scale was less than that of Manchester United. And when we saw Ted in training, we soon realized that he was not as good a player as most of us.

MacDougall was the classic case of a player who moved from club to club and made a lot of money. From Bournemouth, his first club, he went to Manchester United, then West Ham, then Norwich and down to Southampton before rejoining Bournemouth. He never struck me as the coaching type, but to the surprise of most people, he went to Blackpool with Alan Ball as a coach. Moving round the country as he did must have meant a lot of upheaval for his wife and family. It may have been worthwhile financially though there must also have been a real cost in terms of schooling and friendships. It is not something I could have done myself.

Club directors would probably feel exactly the same as players if people in their line of business suddenly started paying themselves higher wages. I do not feel it is fair to accuse players of making excessive demands. It is a short life in football, fifteen or twenty years at the outside, and the natural inclination is to try and earn enough money to make the transition to another livelihood smoother. Relatively high wages help breed a certain lifestyle and it is hard to have to change that and revert to a poorer syle of living at the age of thirty-five. It is easy to say that players have plenty of time to learn a trade or qualify for another profession during their time as footballers and I agree that the opportunities are there, but many players do not bother and it comes as a shock to them when they finally have to quit the game.

The Football League and Professional Footballers' Association have schemes whereby they bear the cost of this training for other jobs, but only a small percentage of players take them up. Much is made of the fact that players can earn money from off-the-field activities, though in my opinion this is greatly exaggerated. Only one player has become rich through commercial activities, England captain Kevin Keegan. And most of his money and connections were made abroad while he was 'European Footballer of the Year' in West Germany.

I would say that an average international player would make up to £5,000 a year from his commercial activities and the average First Division player no more than £1,000. By the time you have paid tax at sixty per cent there is not much left. I realize the ordinary taxpayer will say that everyone has to pay tax, but there is a difference when talking about footballers. Unlike many other high-income earners, they cannot make themselves into companies and have their income channelled into the company so that they can offset expenses against it for tax purposes. The Football League regulations do not allow a player to have his salary paid into a company.

A player can have two or three good years and earn a lot of money in those years only to find that most of it is deducted in tax. He cannot spread the income over a number of years like a writer for instance. And the most important difference of all is that the footballer's career ends at thirty five when his life is only half over.

It is also often said that top players are earning £800 or more a week in basic wages, but again this is an exaggeration. I do not know any personally. When England players get together for matches the subject of wages does come up with certain players, but there is always a tendency to exaggerate. No one wants to give the impression that he is missing out. There was much publicity in the early part of the 1980-81 season about the wages being paid by Aston Villa, who led the First Division table for many weeks. It was claimed that the Villa players earned £250 a point, which meant that if they won two matches in a week, they could receive an extra £1,000 on top of their basic salaries. This was said to have stretched the financial resources of the club – a case of success being a handicap!

I do not know the intricacies of the Aston Villa pay structure, but I would suspect that the £250 a point only applies when Villa are in the top three or near the top of the League. It probably would not apply if they were near the bottom. A number of clubs have a sliding scale of win and draw bonuses which vary according to the club's league position.

Appearance money at most clubs tends to be fairly high for young players who are on the verge of making the first team as an incentive to try and win a regular place. It is lower for established players.

I have seen some players totally bemused by their pay slips at the end of the week because of the variable factors that make up their pay. It reinforces my view that players need a good accountant to ensure they make the best use of their money. Young players can be tempted to spend their money on cars, clothes and discos without bothering to provide for the future. Not many managers will be content to let that happen. The young player will be advised to pay a proportion of his income into a pension fund which is paid out either at the age of thirty-five or on his fortieth birthday. This money is taken from gross income before PAYE is deducted so it is very much in the player's interest to join the scheme.

A player needs to be cushioned against the effects of having to pay tax at the top rate and a sensible accountant will advise him where to invest his money. It is possible for him to be wrongly advised and become over-committed. That is a danger, just as it is risky to go into precarious business ventures. A player has to sort out the cowboys from the genuine people and it is not easy. Many top players have come unstuck in the past.

Freedom of contract has meant that clubs who want to hold on to their more valuable players offer them long-term contracts of four or five, or even ten, years. Before freedom of contract it was rare to have contracts of more than two years. The difficulty about committing oneself to a long-term contract is that inflation can have serious effects on what appeared to be a good wage when the contract was first drawn up. More and more players want some kind of index-linking these days.

Often a player will ask for his contract to be up graded when it still has a year or two to run, and when the matter becomes public knowledge, he is termed greedy and grasping by people who do not know the full facts. Richard Moore, chairman of Derby County, has suggested that there should be a nationally negotiated pay agreement between the Football League and the Professional Footballers' Association, as there is in most industries. He believes that wages are too high and should be reduced. I cannot see this happening. Although football is a team game, it is impossible to bracket everyone in the same pay grade. Football is like show business. There are bound to be some people who can top the bill, whereas others in the same team will never be crowd pullers in the same sense. I can see a further reduction in staff as more and more clubs find difficulty in surviving financially.

The development of the commercial side of the game has been a lifesaver for many clubs. Some of the bigger clubs can make in excess of £½ million a year from this source and many smaller ones only pay their way because of this extra income. But as the recession has bitten deeper, so clubs are realizing that there are limits to what can be brought in from these non-footballing sources. Lotteries, once a very profitable source of revenue, are declining in many areas, particularly those where there is high unemployment. Shirt sponsorship is a potential source of income and the Football League will have to insist that when the next television contract is signed, it is a condition that shirts with advertisements on them can be used in televised games. It seems an anomaly to me that a racing car or tennis player can carry an advertising emblem while a footballer is barred from doing the same thing. There is no such bar on the Continent.

Many people in football say that the television companies should pay much more than they do for the privilege of televising matches. At the moment clubs receive £25,000 a year – a small sum to the Liverpools and Arsenals but a considerable help to the smaller clubs. Perhaps it is possible to insist on higher fees, but I think any increase can only be marginal. There are two factors which should not be overlooked when talking about television. The first is the promotional side. It stimulates interest to see football on television and I do not subscribe to the view that television is killing football. In America no sport is reckoned to have arrived as a major sport until it gets prime-time exposure on television. Soccer has only recently been televised in America and one of my former team mates at West Ham, Phil Woosnam, the Commissioner of the North American Soccer League, is trying desperately to extend the coverage. As we have seen with show jumping, snooker and darts in this country, when a sport has television exposure it becomes more popular.

The danger in England as we enter the 1980s is that there is too much exposure. The television news programmes usually cover the goals of a selected match and with each channel televising three matches every Saturday, it is possible to sit at home on a Saturday night and see the goals of eight matches – eight matches out of forty-six. I feel that is too much. It should not be too difficult to achieve a balance between saturation coverage which has obvious dangers and no televised football at all which would also be harmful to the game. Two matches for each channel every weekend would be just about right. There is a lobby which supports the televising of a live match every Thursday, that match to be withdrawn from the normal Saturday programme. I am opposed to that because I think it could deter people from attending matches.

The second factor in favour of television is an even more valid one, namely the service which television provides those millions of old-age pensioners and disabled people who cannot attend matches. It would be grossly unfair to deprive them of a chance to watch the best football on television. From the players' viewpoint, most of us like to see ourselves on television. It is a way of gaining more notice which might help in advancing our careers.

One way of getting money into the game, it has been suggested, is for the League to run its own football pools. The pools companies have made millions of pounds out of football over the years and doubtless they can be made to contribute much more when their contract with the League ends in 1986. If this happens, the League could insist that the money be used for controlled ground improvements. Whatever extra money is generated within the game, it must be spent wisely. Our stadiums lag behind those in some countries. Many of them need facelifts. Indeed, almost without exception they are old grounds which have been patched up and in some cases they need totally redeveloping. English football needs new grounds with spacious parking, grounds away from crowded town centres, and above all, it needs a new national stadium.

Finally it is worth reminding critics that the amount paid by the Football Association to England players as appearance money has not varied since 1974. Appearance money remains at £100 and when the decline in the value of the pound is taken into account that probably means it is now worth about £40. One of the first steps taken by Don Revie when he became England manager in 1974 was to ask the FA to increase the win and draw bonus and these now stand at £300 for a win and £150 for a draw. I have never heard an England player complain about his remuneration. And come to that, I have never heard a player talk before a game about how much money he stands to make. I never think about money when I play football and I believe that is true of nearly every footballer in the country.

13

Ron and John

Four people have had a great influence over my life – my parents who started me off the right way and encouraged me, and my only two club managers, Ron Greenwood and John Lyall. I was lucky that I grew up near Upton Park and went there to start my footballing career and not to another club. I could have had a dozen managers by now and I could have lived in different parts of the country as many footballers have to when bought and sold.

The absence of dramas and controversies at West Ham suited my temperament. And their ideas about how to play the game suited my style. It is quite possible that I may not have been able to achieve as much as I have done in the game if I had joined another club when I left school. I know I would not have been as happy or contented. Ron Greenwood was always stressing the enjoyable part of football by putting the emphasis on skill and John Lyall is very similar. It is ironic that I should start out under Greenwood and should now be reaching the climax of my international career under him.

Being appointed England manager in 1977 revived his career. He had become very disillusioned about the way English football was going. He thought it was too defensive, too physical and was not producing enough skilful players to compete with the best Continental and South American players. He thought the emphasis in the clubs was too much geared towards competition and pressure instead of technique. Ball-winning and closing down space were looked on as finer virtues than controlling the ball and passing it properly. He felt there was a harsh tone about our game which put us out of step with the rest of the world. He did not belittle the competitiveness of our players. 'If we had more of the Continentals' skill added to our competitiveness we'd beat everyone,' he said.

Taking over from Don Revie, who in many ways was the opposite of him, gave Greenwood the chance to change things, to put the smile back on the face of English football as someone said. He restored wingers and even tried the most adventurous playing system of them all, 4-2-4, against several opponents. Unfortunately his belief in wingers had to be modified when Peter Barnes lost form and was left out of the squad for a time. As there was an acute shortage of wingers, particularly left-sided ones, there was no one else he could draft in and England's system had to be temporarily altered.

Ron Greenwood is totally involved in football. He will talk about it for hours and no other subject will intrude. I have known him for sixteen years yet if someone asked me what his hobbies were outside football I do not know. Football is his hobby. You never read articles about his private life in the newspapers. Away from the game he is a private person, a family man and a church man. When we are on long trips he will rarely discuss current events, only football. He is passionate about it and will remember incidents and moments in matches which he will use to illustrate the point he is making. His footballing memory is unique but he does not use the past to decry the present.

One of the myths which some of his detractors have put forward is that he is too technical for the ordinary player to understand, that he talks above the heads of the players. This is completely untrue. He is always stressing that football is a simple game and adds with a laugh that it is only complicated by some people in it. Simplicity is his constant theme, exhorting us not to over elaborate. He is not a blackboard man. I have never seen him use a blackboard to illustrate a coaching point, nor have I ever seen him use 'Subbuteo' men on a table as some managers do. His blackboard is on the pitch. If he is introducing an idea which some players may not grasp first time he will say: 'Right, let's take it in penny numbers.' In my years with him I have not yet discovered what penny numbers refer to, but what it means is that we first do the exercise at walking pace to make sure everyone knows how to do it. He is happiest when he is working with players out on the training pitch. That is why I believe that the period 1977-80 was the happiest period of his life. Working with the country's best players comes easier to him than the day to day involvement with players at a club.

If Ron had a weakness, I would say it is in handling players, or man management, at club level. Not every player in a club responds the same way to the manager, and during his sixteen years at Upton Park Ron had his problems with one or two players. At club level it is not easy for the manager to move dissident players out quickly. He can be stuck with them for a while. At international level it is simple: you do not invite them back for the next match. With the national side, discipline presents fewer problems because the manager is working with the top players who are usually dedicated otherwise they would not have got where they are in the game. This realization that they could be dropped from the squad acts as the best kind of deterrent to indiscipline. There are also many older players in the present England squad who would jump on a new player if he failed to observe the standards.

After we have gathered on Sunday night at the West Park Lodge Hotel for a mid-week international, Ron will let us go to the local pub for a drink, something Don Revie would never let happen. In my experience, no one has abused that privilege. Self-discipline prevails, not a set of rigid rules. This accords with Ron Greenwood's philosophy that footballers should be treated as grown men and allowed to make their own decisions. Those with what he calls good habits will come through, on and off the field, with some degree of success.

Ron Greenwood liked being England manager more than being a club manager because his strength is the football and coaching side, and working with the players. The other side, the arguing with players about money and contracts, was less appealing to him. John Lyall, in contrast, does not mind this aspect of his job. Although he shares most of Greenwood's beliefs about the game he differs from him in one important aspect – handling players. There is a harder edge about John. If he has to tell a young professional that he is not going to be a success he will willingly do it, but in a nice way. Man management is one of his strengths.

During his time at West Ham, Ron had to strive to achieve some kind of balance between sticking to his attacking beliefs and getting results. When the team was not playing well the temptation was there to pull more players back and tighten up defensively, which most managers would have done. He refused to do this. In the years when we were fighting relegation, we were still encouraged to attack. We were criticized for being too slack defensively and that was probably true. Ron's forte was working with expressive, attacking players. Most of our troubles came in defence, particularly in the air.

John Lyall's principles are slightly different. He wants flair in attack, but also consistency in defence which is why he changed the staff round two years ago and bought in players such as Phil Parkes, Ray Stewart, Alvin Martin and Paul Allen. The change was noticed more away from home than at Upton Park. Whereas before we might go to Preston or Blackburn and impress people with our attacking ability as we lost, we would now go to places like that and battle for a 0-0 draw if that was the best result we could achieve on the day. The joke at Upton Park is that John Lyall has put steel rods up our backs.

There is always humour and laughter in any football club and there is certainly plenty of it at West Ham. Ron Greenwood has a good sense of humour, not in the sharp, barbed one-line style of a Tommy Docherty but in a friendly, mickey-taking way. When we were doing shooting practices his favourite dig at me was 'Got your handbag with you this morning?' I have never seen him lose his temper. In that respect, he resembles Alf Ramsey. Even at half time when games were not going well, he could still keep reasonably calm. One of his great strengths is to pick out weaknesses in the opposition during matches and get his own team to exploit them. I remember in a Football League Cup semi-final tie at Stoke he picked out the left side of their defence as the side to attack. Harry Redknapp, our right winger at the time, was fed the ball constantly and most of our threatening moves came from that side. Before England's World Cup game in Belfast in 1979 he asked us to by-pass

midfield and get the early balls up to the front players Trevor
Francis and Tony Woodcock because he felt Northern Ireland's
back four of Pat Rice, Allan Hunter, Jimmy Nicholl and
Sammy Nelson lacked pace. It was a considerable change of
style – Fourth Division stuff – but it worked. Francis and
Woodcock each scored twice and we won 5-1.

The previous year in Denmark his advice was to stick as
many high balls in as possible because the Danes were weak in
the air. Again it worked but only just because we won 4-3. Ron
Greenwood is not the kind of coach to overload players with
unnecessary advice. Most of his instructions are short and
simple. Basically he wants players to make their own decisions.
He expects them to be intelligent enough to examine the
possibilities and decide for themselves. You will never see a
player under Ron Greenwood turning and looking to the
sidelines for help. A Greenwood team has not been
programmed to play in a certain way.

Nowadays, most top managers have an assistant to help
them. Such partnerships have included Brian Clough and Peter
Taylor, John Barnwell and Ritchie Barker, Terry Neill and
Don Howe, Keith Burkinshaw and Peter Shreeves, Ron
Atkinson and Mick Brown, Bobby Robson and Bobby
Ferguson and Alan Mullery and Ken Craggs. But Ron
Greenwood is very much his own man and away from the
England set-up he will not usually be seen travelling with a
favourite aide.

Under Ramsey, England was a one-man band. Under Revie
it was a duet with Revie and Les Cocker. Under Greenwood, it
is a team with six coaches responsible to him – Bobby Robson,
Don Howe, Dave Sexton, Terry Venables, Geoff Hurst and Bill
Taylor. This three-tier system, with the England 'B' and
Under-21 sides each having a manager and coach, is
undoubtedly the best way of running a nation's football teams.
It is more than a one-man job and Greenwood delegates
responsibility to the people under him without having any one
particular confidante.

If there is one man who has probably had more influence over
Ron Greenwood than any other it is Walter Winterbottom, the
first England manager after World War II and the founder of

the FA Coaching scheme. They are firm friends and have similar ideas. Both have immense reputations abroad within football. Ron's work on FIFA study groups before he became England manager probably made him England's leading expert on world football when he succeeded Don Revie. He has travelled to most of the leading footballing countries and is an avid reader of the foreign footballing press.

Like many outstanding coaches, Ron Greenwood was not a player who gained international recognition. He was an intelligent and authoritative centre-half who was good enough to gain one England 'B' cap. Born in Burnley, he played for Bradford Park Avenue, Brentford, Chelsea, whom he helped win the League Championship in 1954-55, and Fulham. He coached Oxford University, Walthamstow Avenue and Eastbourne United before becoming Arsenal's assistant manager and coach in 1958. Three years later he took over from Ted Fenton at West Ham and later became manager of England's Under-23 team.

I have never known him say before a match 'We'll have to play this one tight and aim for a draw', not even when West Ham have been playing at Anfield or Old Trafford. His team talk was always about trying to win, about being positive and about scoring goals. He encourages players to contribute ideas to discussions. And he will never knock a good idea down, whoever it comes from.

To suggest, as the newspapers did on the morning of the England v Scotland match at Wembley on 23 May 1981, that Ron had bowed to 'player power' was simply untrue. The players were amazed when we read the reports and we could understand Ron being annoyed. It was said that the players had persuaded him to drop Peter Barnes, one of the successes against the Brazilians a short time before. I was at the team meeting the previous Thursday which followed the disappointing 0-0 draw against Wales, and none of us mentioned Peter by name. With the Switzerland and Hungary World Cup games imminent, Ron asked us how we saw the midfield and whether we felt we should have three specialist midfield players instead of a withdrawn winger or a forward playing a little deeper. With the World Cup games in mind, the concensus of opinion was in favour of a specialist midfield and we assumed that, if Ron agreed with us, Glenn Hoddle, Butch Wilkins and Graham Rix would be the three.

None of us had any idea of the team until Ron announced it the next day. It was his team, not ours. The fact that the newspapers all had the same line suggested there had been some collusion. If one reporter had misinterpreted what Ron had said it would not have been so bad, but they all did. When England lost 0-1 to Scotland, rather unluckily because the incident when Trevor Francis was fouled was just as much a penalty as the Bryan Robson trip on Steve Archibald, Ron's mood did not improve and it came as no surprise when we heard he had walked out of his press conference after the game.

Like me, John Lyall has a father who was a policeman. Both his parents were Scots, although he was born and bred in the East End. I think that says something about his character. He is a grafter, a disciplinarian and a man who believes passionately in the good things of football. He summed up his approach in an interview with Hugh McIlvanney, the Scottish sports columnist of *The Observer* in which he said:

My attitude to football is that I have to try to get players to play with style and pride. I know I'll admire them if they do that and so will most of the people watching them.

If we can get the supporters up off their seats half a dozen times a game for some reason we're doing the job right. One would love it to be goals that got them up cheering but if it's because of a beautiful build up or because a fella goes past four players and hits the post then that's not bad.

There must always be something beyond mere effectiveness in the game, there must be a dream. I think if I had been allowed to be any one player for a day it would have been Georgie Best. There's a mystique about the game that we have to maintain and we're lucky here at West Ham that we have players who can help to do that.

He picked me out as an example. 'The standards he sets affect the others around him,' he said. It is a team effort really, producing a brand of football which was developed in the era of

Greenwood and which continues to delight one of the most loyal crowds in the country. The fans keep going back because they know that there will be times during almost every match when they will be pulled out of their seats.

As a player, John Lyall never gave less than one hundred per cent, which was probably why he was seriously injured and had to quit. I never played with him but I watched him as an apprentice. He was a hard player and a fearless tackler. He still plays in training games with us but mainly in five-a-sides using one or two touches, as his knee will not stand up to games that demand twisting and turning. He trains the players hard, harder than Ron Greenwood, but as with his mentor, he concentrates on ball work. Most of our running is done with the ball and the routines are interesting and stimulating. Training is never boring at Chadwell Heath, our training ground.

John Lyall shares one outstanding quality with Ron Greenwood: he is an intensely honest man. You will not find him ducking or diving to avoid telling the truth. If a player is not doing what he wants, he will tell him to his face. You know where you are with him. He is also very approachable. At training he is one of the lads, laughing and joking with everyone else. But at all times the players know who is in charge. If they overstep the mark they can be in trouble. When he has to be, John Lyall can be a hard man. No footballer would ever want it different. Discipline is a vital part of a football club, so is respect, and I know all of us respect him.

Lyall shares another managerial quality with Greenwood: his dislike of public controversy. He does not talk to the press with headlines in mind. His feeling is that the image of the club has to be preserved so he has to think about what he is saying before he says it. I wish some other managers were the same.

It is a coincidence, I think, that so many good coaches and managers such as John Bond, Noel Cantwell, Ken Brown, Malcolm Allison, Dave Sexton and Andy Nelson came from Upton Park. Most of them were there before Greenwood's arrival in 1961 so they cannot be considered followers of the Greenwood philosophy. John Lyall came later and is more of a Greenwood man. He has taken the best of Greenwood's beliefs and added a few of his own.

The snag with aiming for brilliance all the time is that it breeds inconsistency. It is impossible to hit a peak every week. John has tried to overcome this by continuing to encourage West Ham to attack, but at the same time making sure that fewer mistakes are made in defence. He believes that the basis of a good side is a solid defence, and this added to West Ham's attacking flair has made us a successful club again.

14

Managers

One job I will not be taking up when I retire from playing is managing a football club. I have some of the qualifications needed, including an FA Full Badge and a fair amount of business training, but it is not the career for me. It is too precarious, even more so than being a player.

Before the 1980-81 season was half over, six clubs that finished in the bottom half of the First Division the previous season had changed their manager. The manager I feel particularly sorry for was Ian Greaves who lost his job at Bolton. Ian nearly brought Bolton up from the Second Division in successive seasons and when he eventually succeeded he was sacked because the team had a bad season. A good manager had, in the eyes of the Burden Park fans and the directors, become a bad manager which of course was nonsense. The problem with a club such as Bolton is that it will always struggle because it is short of money and is limited in crowd potential with the Manchester clubs and Liverpool so accessible. However, I was pleased to see him back in the game within a year as manager of Oxford United.

Bristol City, another club to be relegated at the end of the 1979-80 season, also yielded to crowd pressure and Alan Dicks, the longest serving manager in the Football League, found himself out of a job. There are countless instances of managers being sacrificed, yet for every manager sacked, there are twenty or thirty people waiting to step into his job. Often the manager who is dismissed does not have his contract paid up and sits at home, continuing to draw his basic salary, while his solicitor contests settlement with the club. In one extreme case,

Portsmouth were paying three managers at the same time, the existing manager plus two previous managers who had been sacked. George Petchey was a typical example when he left Millwall. As Millwall had severe financial problems, he was forced to see off several of his best young players. Yet when he was told he had to leave, the club did not have enough money to settle his contract.

Petchey was replaced by Peter Anderson, the former Luton, Sheffield United, Anderlecht and Tampa Bay Rowdies forward who had no previous managerial experience. Though I think the methods of selection need improving with more emphasis placed on qualifications and some form of experience, it is possible for a player to become a manager overnight and be successful. It can be done if the person concerned has the qualities needed for management.

Such a person was Alan Mullery who had no managerial experience when he took over at Brighton in July 1976. After retiring as a player at Fulham, he was out of the game for several weeks and frustrated at being unable to get a coaching or managerial post when Brighton chairman Mike Bamber contacted him. Mullery's forceful personality took Brighton out of the Third Division the following year and two years later, he took the team into the First Division for the first time in the club's history. Mullery proved that previous managerial experience was not always essential. When he quit Brighton in June 1981, he was the forty-second manager to leave his club in ten months – an incredible turn over!

Someone I thought would emulate Mullery was Frank McLintock. Whenever I played against him, Frank was the man who pulled the strings in the other side. He was an outstanding captain and leader and seemed ideally suited to instant management. But in his brief spell at Leicester success eluded him and he resigned. Living in London where he had business interests and driving up and down the motorway was given as the chief reason why he failed. Perhaps he realized that management is a hazardous life and was provident enough to have something to fall back on when it did go wrong. Much as I would like to see him back in football, I cannot see Frank having a second chance of being a manager. Players will be wondering about what went wrong at Filbert Street. Players are the key people. The manager has to have their respect. If they have any doubts in him, his chances of survival are diminished.

The business of plucking a player from the ranks and making him the boss is very much a hit and miss affair. Far better if the candidate has had some experience at a lower level, as Geoff Hurst had at Telford United before he became manager of Chelsea. Or even coaching experience, which Terry Venables had at Crystal Palace before he succeeded Malcolm Allison as manager. John Lyall had what I consider the ideal apprenticeship at West Ham. When he was forced to retire from playing at the age of twenty-three through a bad knee, he worked for a time in the club offices handling wages and accounts. At the same time he started coaching the younger players. Soon he gave up office work and concentrated full time on coaching under Ron Greenwood. In 1971 he became assistant manager and had three years valuable experience before taking over as club manager in 1974. In all, he had had seven years to learn the job. He knew the players and the players knew him. He also knew the system at West Ham. It was a natural progression. Not many clubs are patient enough to want to copy the West Ham example.

Running a football club is now such a huge responsibility that I believe it is beyond the powers of one man to do it properly. Some still do the job as a one-man band, and Bobby Robson at Ipswich is perhaps the outstanding example, because although he has a coaching staff to support him the buck definitely stops at his desk. I think it is time we copied the Continental system and divided the job into two parts, a team manager who looks after the playing side and a general manager who is responsible for the financial aspects. It is too much to expect the manager to argue with a player about a contract and then next day ask him to play for him in a vital match. A rift may have opened between them. If the dispute is between the player and the general manager it is the general manager who is cast as the baddie. The team manager still has the confidence of the player.

QPR are one club who operate this system with great success. Venables runs the playing side and Jim Gregory, the club chairman, is in charge of finance. Some managers will try to placate players by saying: 'I've passed your request on to the board.' But once they say that they weaken their position. Any manager who enjoys the full support of his directors knows he has to answer the players himself. The directors only ratify what he decides. This problem could be eased with the introduction of the paid managing director at football clubs. This idea was voted for by the clubs, only for the FA to reject it at their annual meeting in May 1981.

At present the successful manager must have a number of assets which are denied most players in football. Firstly, he must know the game and needs to be a good coach, preferably with the Full Badge. He must command respect and have the ruthlessness to sack people. He must also be a good businessman, although there are few in this category, and a good public relations officer for his club. I think players will respond more to a manager who is honest in his approach. I do not agree with Tommy Docherty that a manager has to be a liar and a cheat. Few have fulfilled all these requirements satisfactorily. Instead, there are types of managers who excel in certain areas. The number one motivator is undoubtedly Brian Clough, although I have said before that I would not like to work for him. He is much too abrasive in style for me. Some players might respond to him but I would not.

The manager plays a very important part in making a team a winning side, but there has been a tendency in recent years to overplay this part. The name of the manager now looms larger than the team or the club. Whatever the manager does or says, it is what the eleven players do once a game starts that decides the fortunes of the club. Players are still more important than managers. Managers do not score winning goals.

A good manager, however, can transform a struggling club as John Bond has done at Manchester City since taking over from Malcolm Allison. Before his arrival, City had just three points and appeared doomed to go down into the Second Division. Yet under Bond's positive style of management, they soon shot up the table to safety and took part in a memorable FA Cup final. There was no mass clear out of players and only three new ones were bought. Allison had to admit that at least one of them, Tommy Hutchison, was the type of player City had needed and was a sound investment.

Allison's televised attack on Bond was one of the worst examples of one manager criticizing another. It was unfounded and grossly unfair. He said that Bond had never produced a good side in his life and was only winning matches at Manchester City because he had been left a good squad of players. Allison implied that if he had had more time at Maine Road, the club would eventually have been successful. This could never be proved and I think it is bad for the image of the game when managers say such things in public. There is too much harsh criticism expressed by managers and I feel it has contributed to the low opinion that many people now have of the national sport. Allan Clarke is another example of a manager speaking out unneccessarily. In his first year of management he weighed in with a number of extreme views about Ron Greenwood, other managers and hooliganism – flog them in front of the stand, he said – and generally succeeded in damaging the game. Clarke was not one of my favourite opponents when he played for Leeds, and when he became manager at Elland Road he did nothing to alter my opinion of him. There needs to be more restraint in this area. Too many managers, I feel, are seeking to project themselves at the expense of the game.

One essential qualtiy needed by a manager is the ability to handle people and outstanding in this is Lawrie McMenemy of Southampton. I have never worked with him, but I imagine he is easy to talk to and a ready listener. Although he enjoys a good relationship with his players, they respect him as the boss at the Dell.

Ron Saunders of Aston Villa is perhaps the leading figure in the old-fashioned school of management, a hard taskmaster who insists on stern discipline and maximum effort at all times. Now that the Villa boardroom troubles are over, he has set about making Villa one of the most successful clubs in the League again. Most of his players are in their early twenties and it is players in this age group who most readily respond to his type of management. Older, more confident players with pride in their ability might resent his methods. I felt this was the case during his short reign at Manchester City. Ron Saunders is a grafter himself and expects everyone else to work hard too. He is the modern equivalent of Stan Cullis, the man who made Wolves a top side in the 1950s.

Bob Paisley has similar qualities at Liverpool although he is more of an uncle figure than a strict schoolmaster. Bob subscribes to the same old-fashioned virtues as Saunders – reliability, hardwork and common sense. He believes in getting good players round him and letting them play to a simple, uncomplicated pattern. For all his success, Liverpool cannot be talked about as Paisley's team in the way Ipswich can be talked about as Bobby Robson's team or Villa Ron Saunders' team. Liverpool rely on complete teamwork – from chairman John Smith and secretary Peter Robinson to the members of the backroom staff. There are few better chairmen than Smith in the Football League nor many better secretaries than Robinson. Paisley is not an FA Coach himself and does not believe that good players need too much coaching.

To an extent, I agree with him. I do not think an international player needs to be taught how to pass the ball, but he can be helped to improve his strengths and make better use of his talents. At top level, the manager and his staff should concentrate on building up fitness and team understanding. The development of attacking moves is largely instinctive – the good habits of players coming out in a positive way. If everything was rehearsed, a counter could be devised by rival coaches. The bulk of attacking moves has to be improvised.

One of the chief merits of attending the FA's summer coaching courses is that it encourages participants to speak in public. Not many footballers are shy, but addressing a meeting and putting their ideas over is not one of their strong points. To become a qualified coach, it is necessary to be able to speak lucidly. Without this art, a manager is lost. Some people will be able to pass examinations at Lilleshall and Bisham Abbey by learning what they are told and repeating it parrot fashion. But the main emphasis is on an exchange of views and making players think about the game. Two aspiring managers who attended the course I went to were Ken Knighton and Frank Clarke who later became manager and assistant manager of Sunderland. It was clear from the start that they had a good relationship and I feel this is another important part of managerial success. The manager needs a reliable partner who thinks along similar lines.

Terry Neill and Don Howe are an ideal partnership at Arsenal. Don is the coach and disciplinarian while Terry is the amiable front man who takes the pressures of management. Perhaps the outstanding example of a manager who believes fervently in coaching is Dave Sexton at Coventry City. Dave's main strength is as a coach and tactician and it was feared that when he was with his previous club, Manchester United, he would have problems because the job there needs a showman and extrovert as much as a coach. Yet Dave appeared to prove most people wrong and had carried out the job with quiet dignity until his unfortunate dismissal in summer 1981.

In the main, managers are big men. It helps to have a commanding presence in the McMenemy-Allison-Bond mould, but personality is the key. One of the big-men type managers is Ron Atkinson of Manchester United, a flamboyant character who likes being in the limelight. He knows what players think and what motivates them. His ideas about the game are sound and it is not surprising that Albion challenged for honours after his arrival at the Hawthorns.

As a player you sometimes meet another player who you think will become a leading manager and I must say I felt that way when Bobby Gould first came to Upton Park. He had a lively, uplifting personality and knew how to encourage people and make them more contented. He could always laugh and joke even when the team was losing. Such enthusiasm is rare and I was not surprised when Geoff Hurst asked him to become his assistant at Chelsea. They had met on a coaching course and like Knighton and Clarke, had formed a firm relationship. Although Bobby had his problems at Chelsea I am sure he will emerge as a strong personality in the future.

Graham Taylor of Watford has always impressed me and I can see him becoming one of the top managers in the game. He organizes his players well and works them hard. Whenever West Ham have played Watford we have known it will be a hard, relentless game. I have wondered why Watford did not make more impact in the Second Division. It is not a Division that is packed with good sides. But success could come in the next year or so at Vicarage Road. Graham is one of the best communicators in the game, a good talker who is full of ideas. Watford chairman Elton John made the right move when he offered him a further five year contract. Crystal Palace wanted Graham when Terry Venables resigned and I have no doubt that he would have revitalised Palace had he gone to Selhurst Park.

Two more younger managers who I feel will go on to become successful in the game are Howard Kendall and Graham Turner who started as player managers of Blackburn Rovers and Shrewsbury Town respectively. It is difficult enough being a manager without also playing, but these two coped very well. Kendall transformed Blackburn when he took charge, quickly making them one of the best sides in the Division. Having missed promotion on a goal difference, Howard returned to his old club Everton and it will be interesting to see how he handles the extra pressure that automatically comes with a club of such tradition and demands success.

Turner has been manager at Shrewsbury three years and with little cash has managed to keep them in the Second Division. He impresses me as a very sound and reliable person. Probably the Second Division's most exciting young newcomer, however, is John Toshack who at thirty-two is one of the youngest managers in the game. Since 1978 Toshack has taken Swansea from the Fourth Division to the First and revitalized a famous old club. He has shown himself to be an astute tactician who is confident enough in his own ideas to introduce radical changes. When West Ham played Swansea, he pushed the full-backs into midfield and played three centre-backs in the centre of defence. It was difficult to get past them. He too, was a player manager which proves that some very exceptional people can do both jobs. There are a number of success stories in management but they are far outnumbered by the failures.

In West Germany coaches have to serve a three-year period of apprenticeship before they are granted a licence to manage a club in the Bundesliga. It is impossible to become an instant manager without qualifications. A system like that would stop the Mullerys and Toshacks moving into management, but it has the merit of ensuring managers have proper training. Managers are still sacked in West Germany because not every team can be successful.

A better form of managerial training than the haphazard way we have here must benefit the game. It would probably reduce the number of sackings. If the methods of selection were sounder, the number of managers incapable of doing the job would fall.

The Football League chairmen reached an agreement not to poach each other's managers during a season, and at the time this seemed to be a good idea. In fact all it succeeded in doing was to condense the managerial sackings into a short period at the end of the season. It failed to stop the poaching: unofficial tapping continued and in fact there were more managerial changes than ever before as clubs panicked into hasty decisions before the new season began.

15

Playing in Europe

West Ham made headlines in October 1980 when they became
the first English club to be instructed to stage a European match
behind closed doors because of the misbehaviour of the club's
supporters before and during the first leg of the first round tie
against Castilla in Madrid on 17 September. UEFA at first
ordered West Ham to play their next two home matches in the
European Cup Winners Cup 300 kilometres (about 180 miles)
away from Upton Park. However, the club appealed and the
penalty was amended so that the second leg at Upton Park could
only be played in front of club officials, the UEFA
representatives and the press – a total of 262 people. As a crowd
of more than 30,000 was expected that meant the club was being
fined over £50,000 which would have been the takings. In the
European Cup Winners Cup the home club keeps its own
receipts. Most of the players were sceptical about having to play
in an empty ghost-like stadium and many felt it would be better
to play at Sunderland where there would have been a
reasonable-sized crowd. Having lost 1-3 to Castilla, Real
Madrid's nursery side, in the Bernabeu Stadium, we were
worried that the lack of atmosphere might count against us and
we would go out of the competition.

As it turned out our fears were unfounded, but there was a
time in the second half when we wished there had been a crowd.
We led 3-0 at halftime and then Castilla scored with a thirty-
yard shot to make the score level on aggregate. That would have
been the ideal time for supporters to have lifted the players.
Instead the only noise we heard above the sound of the radio
commentators was the fog-horn voice of Eddie Baily, the club's

chief scout and number one 'gee-up' man. A veteran of World War II, most of Eddie's exhortations are related to the use of the bayonet, and he can be scathing if he thinks someone has pulled out of a tackle. He is also very severe on those players he believes could work harder. It was the first time in my footballing experience that I could hear everything that was said from the bench. Normally in a match the manager, or coach, will shout at his players only for his cries to be lost in the roar of the crowd. I often wonder why coaches do so much shouting as usually it is a waste of their energy.

We failed to score again in the second half, but went through to the second round with two goals in extra time to make the aggregate score 6-4. David Cross was very sharp that night, scoring three of the goals.

There had been fears that thousands of supporters might turn up outside the ground and force their way in as had happened many years ago when a Cup game was ordered to be played on a neutral ground and the fans excluded. A number of public appeals to fans to stay away seemed to have worked and to make sure, there were police officers strategically placed outside to turn supporters away. The story had a happy ending but it did not look that way after the happenings in Madrid.

The players did not learn of the crowd trouble until after the game and we still do not know whether it was exaggerated or as bad as the UEFA evidence claimed it had been. The players are usually the last people to know about the causes and effects of crowd violence. It seemed indisputable from the evidence that some young West Ham fans urinated over a balcony on to some Spanish supporters and I can understand that provoking the police into action. But as often happens in such situations, guilty and innocent alike were struck as the Spanish police waded in. English supporters are used to being dealt with in a much more civilized manner by their own police and it came as a shock to our fans to be attacked in this way. The saddest incident of all, however, was the death of a young West Ham fan after he had been run down outside the stadium.

I am sure that the availabilty of wine which is cheap and plentiful in Madrid was a major contributory cause of the disturbances. I saw a number of youngsters under the influence of drink as we arrived at the ground. In their state it was likely that there would be trouble. English and Scottish clubs are being forced to ban the sale of alcohol inside their grounds, but as the Castilla affair showed, the trouble comes after young supporters have been drinking all day. It is possible to prevent this when the fans are in organized parties and do not arrive until late in the day. West Ham went to considerable lengths to make sure the fans that made the trip were under supervision and accountable to responsible officials. However, there was nothing to stop people who were on holiday in Spain at the time going to the game and probably it was the fans who made their own way who caused the disturbances. While it is easy to say ban all English fans from making trips with football clubs, how does one stop those who make their own way? This is a problem the game has to live with and meanwhile our reputation in Europe diminishes each time there are incidents.

There was no crowd trouble on our next trip, to the Romanian club Poli Timisoara, for the simple reason that only a handful of our fans wanted to go – trips behind the Iron Curtain are very depressing. The Romanians were a better side than their 4-0 defeat at Upton Park indicated and we were thankful we had such a big lead when we played at their stadium.

Despite all the problems, I am very much in favour of English clubs playing in Europe. The strength of our club football is reflected in our success in the three major European competitions and there is no doubt that clubs such as Liverpool and Nottingham Forest have gained in stature and experience through their years in Europe. They have also become richer.

Having a run in a European competition is good for the players because it means they gain more recognition, and a player who is in the public eye is more likely to win international honours than one who is not. Most of the national newspapers send reporters on these trips and so do BBC Sound Radio, Independent Radio News and occasionally BBC television and ITV. There is always a snippet of film shown the following Saturday and the club generally gets more coverage in the media than normal.

Foreign travel is an exciting experience for the players and provides a chance to go to some interesting places that are not on the tourist map. Such a place is Erevan in the Soviet Republic of Armenia near the Turkish-Iranian border. We went there in the European Cup Winners Cup in 1975 drawing 1-1 and winning the second leg 3-1 at home. Aeroflot, the Soviet airline, provided us with some of the shakiest landings we have ever encountered, firstly in below-zero temperatures at Moscow and then 1,500 miles south in the 75-degree heat of Erevan. The long, punishing trip gave us some impression of the vastness of the Soviet Union and it also confirmed our misgivings about the Communist way of life. We were given some spending money to buy presents, but after touring the main shopping areas we returned to our fourteen-storey hotel without having made a single purchase. There was nothing to buy! The drab goods were laid out on the counters like a jumble sale.

Our hotel rooms were full of cockroaches and catching them helped while away the time. The curtains in my room were full of holes and on each floor of the hotel was a forbidding middle-aged matron-type lady who looked after the keys and ensured there were no unwelcome guests. Erevan is not far from Mount Ararat where Noah's Ark was supposed to have landed. As it meant crossing the border into Turkey, we did not go on the sightseeing trip.

I did not even make the trip on to the pitch at the 77,000 all-seated stadium. The morning before the match I went down with a stomach virus which was to recur on five separate occasions during the next two months. This was despite the club taking all their own food, including steaks, vegetables and chocolate gateaux. I did not drink any water so I could not understand how I became ill.

Pat Holland took over the number 11 shirt and had a fine game. So did John McDowell, who played alongside Tommy Taylor in defence. Alan Taylor scored first in the fifty-sixth minute to still the noise of the crowd. Ten minutes later Erevan equalized with a goal that would never have been allowed in England. Mervyn Day went up for a high ball, was fouled and the ball ran loose. A defender played it back to him and he was standing with it in his hands when Samuel Petrosian headed it out of his hands and knocked it over the line. The packed audience jumped to their feet throwing torn programmes into the air and letting off firecrackers. Fortunately there were no more Erevan goals and we were able to set off for the airport unmolested.

I was still unwell when the first leg of the next round took place in The Hague against the Dutch club Den Haag. Two of the goals in our 2-4 defeat came from disputed penalties and the fourth was quite bizarre even by European standards. The East German referee Rudi Glockner, who refereed the 1970 World Cup final, stopped the game in the forty-first minute when a bottle was hurled in the direction of Mervyn Day. Lex Schoenmaker, one of the Den Haag players, went behind the goal to appeal to the fans to behave and Glockner re-started the game with a dropped ball on the centre circle. As Graham Paddon went to dispute possession with Schoenmaker Herr Glockner waved him back and Schoenmaker had no opposition as he gained control of the ball and set off for goal. He finished off by placing the ball past Day to make the score 0-4 at half-time.

The most amazing incident of all came when Glockner stopped the game and said he would not continue until Kevin Lock pulled his socks up. Even Ron Greenwood was upset about that. 'The referee told me this was a FIFA ruling and was the custom in East Germany' he said. 'It may happen in a Communist state but it doesn't happen in the free world.' Kevin had to pull his socks up and put on his tie ups. Several West Ham players used to play with their socks down around this time, including Billy Bonds, Graham Paddon and Frank Lampard.

Two second-half goals from Billy Jennings made it a more respectable 2-4. West Ham won the second leg 3-1 and as the aggregate score was then 5-5 we went through the fourth round on the away goals rule. Our semi-final opponents were the West German side Eintracht Frankfurt. It was a relief after the rigours of Erevan and the controversies of Den Haag to go to an orderly place like Frankfurt where we could expect an entertaining game untrammelled by bottle-throwing crowds and generally pedantic East German referees.

Eintracht, who had World Cup stars Bernd Hölzenbein and Jurgen Grabowski in their side, were the best team we played in

One of the more pleasant assignments among my promotional activities was a day out with Pan's People. Perhaps it is too cold in this country, but it is surprising that the American-style cheer leaders have not caught on here although Bristol City tried the idea.

With my West Ham midfield partner Alan Devonshire. A former fork-lift truck driver and part-timer with Southall, Alan made a late start to his career but soon overtook most of his rivals. His two England caps in 1980 will, I suspect, be the first of many.

The most memorable goal of my life – the only one in the 1980 FA Cup Final. Stua
Pearson has miss-hit a shot and I have bent backwards to head past Pat Jennings. Noti
how Arsenal had two men on the goal-line: John Devine (far post) and David Price (ne
post) although it wasn't a corner or a free kick. Defensively they are one of the bes
organised sides in England.

Tackled by Arsenal's Graham Rix at Wembley. Although a forward, Graham probat
gets more tackles in during a match than the average defender. Stuart Pearson is behir
Graham with Billy Bonds on the left. (*Photo*: The Press Association)

I am very much involved with helping those less fortunate than myself.

The Brooking family at home at Brentwood. Having a happy, settled family life is bonus for any man, especially a footballer. (*Photo*: Monte Fresco)

The joy that comes from scoring! Peter Barnes congratulates me after I scored England's second in the 2- victory over the Italians i 1977.

the competition. They were typically German with all their players equally good in attack as in defence. It needed a spectacular thirty-yard goal from Graham Paddon to give us a presentable 1-2 scoreline to take back to Upton Park. Paddon played on the left that day with Billy Bonds in the middle and me on the right. It was a good trio, well balanced and skilled. I thought Graham was a very effective player for West Ham and regretted when he was sold back to Norwich. Shortly after moving he broke a leg and was out of the game for a long time. The return match still provides one of my favourite memories. I scored twice, once with my head, in our 3-1 victory, to give us a place in the final against the Belgian side Anderlecht. We needed a lift because after being League leaders on 8 November we failed to win a single game in our last sixteen and finished the season in eighteenth position.

The fact that the final was played in Anderlecht's Heysel Stadium in front of 58,000 fans was a big advantage to our opponents but we still could have repeated our 1965 success in the competition. We led 1-0 through Patsy Holland before Frank Lampard had to retire with a groin strain. Later, he needed a pelvic operation and was out for some months. John McDowell had to move to full-back with Holland coming into midfield and Alan Taylor substituting for Lampard. Keith Robson scored a second goal, but Rensenbrink and Van der Elst, Anderlecht's Dutch and Belgian internationals, scored two goals each to make the final score 2-4. Rensenbrink and Van der Elst had exceptional pace and Rensenbrink was one of the best flank strikers I have ever seen. He gave Keith Coleman a hard time and Tommy Taylor was equally stretched by Van der Elst.

My abiding memory of Brussels was the high cost of living. Unlike in the Soviet Union, in Brussels there were all kinds of presents to buy although at prohibitively high prices. Perhaps one of the most pleasant trips of that European campaign was to Finland for the first round game against Reipas Lahden. With a Finnish wife loyalties were a bit strained. The Finns were exceptionally friendly and we enjoyed our fleeting visit.

Undoubtedly the worst trip abroad I have ever been on was to Tbilisi, Georgia in March 1981. It was a nightmare from start to finish. None of us was keen to go because the tie had virtually been decided in the first leg at Upton Park when Dinamo Tbilisi surprised us with their technical skills and finishing and won 4-1. Our crowd gave them a standing ovation as they left the pitch, proving once again that the West Ham fans know their football and are ready to applaud the good things of the game. I thought Dinamo were one of the best club sides I had ever seen. I was particularly impressed with the way they kept possession under pressure and waited for an opportunity to hit long balls to their strikers who played wide on the flanks.

Not having a centre-forward to mark meant that Billy Bonds had to move up into midfield. These tactics took us by surprise because we had been told that Dinamo worked the ball forward patiently through midfield. At least it proved that there is no substitute for spying on opponents yourself instead of relying on the advice of other managers! Unfortunately we were not able to watch Dinamo in advance because their domestic season had closed. In the dressing room afterwards the general feeling was that even though we had had a bad night and given away sloppy goals, Dinamo were still a class or two above any other side we had met in the competition. David Cross said that if we had to meet teams like that every week he would announce his retirement!

Our flight from Stansted to Tbilisi two weeks later was at nine in the morning which meant an early rise. The Aeroflot Turpolev 134 – not one of the world's best-appointed passenger aircraft – was scheduled to stop at Riga in Latvia to refuel and also in Moscow for customs checks before flying on to Tbilisi, a city of one million inhabitants near the Iranian border. The total distance was 4,000 miles – a tortuous roundabout route which might have been considerably reduced had we been able to avoid Moscow.

In fact, we had enough fuel to make Moscow direct so we did not need to land in Riga. We arrived at Moscow's impressive, marble-floored airport at 2.35 English time and we were to get to know it intimately in the next eight hours. The temperature was minus 16 degrees Fahrenheit and the snow was piled up in huge drifts around the airport buildings. The process of passing through security, immigration and customs and then coming back through security, immigration and customs took four hours. Although we were to use the same plane for the second half of the trip, the luggage had to be taken out of the hold and inspected. At 6.30 we heard that there was a possibility that the plane might not be able to take off because of the blizzards. For nearly two hours we were kept in a sparse departure lounge without refeshments and the explanation was that having been cleared by security, we couldn't get back out again. After stopping overnight at a spartan transit hotel, it was lunchtime, 12.20, the next day when we at last took off for the 1,500-mile flight to Tbilisi and we were all very relieved to escape from Moscow. Our reception in Georgia's ancient city of Tbilisi (it is a city which dates back 1,500 years) was in complete contrast. The temperature was fifty degrees higher and there was a welcoming committee on the tarmac to greet us. Apparently their officials had been at the airport all night and were cursing the Moscovites as heartily as we had done. Although Georgia is one of the fifteen republics of the USSR, the inhabitants there are not well disposed towards the Russians.

The game against Dinamo the next night must have been an anti-climax for the 80,000 all-seated fans who had paid up to £1.50 for the best seats. Dinamo were much less effective in their finishing than they had been two weeks earlier and after they had wasted several opportunities, Stuart Pearson came on in the 65th minute and volleyed a spectacular goal from David Cross's right-wing centre to give us a 1-0 victory. With all the travelling and delays most of us were very tired by the end.

The plane was supposed to be waiting at the airport for us to make a speedy departure for Moscow but when we arrived we were told it was still in Moscow two-and-a-half hours flying-time away! Billy Bonds and I settled down to play cards in our usual school and Pat Doran, the club caterer, made the time pass more quickly by serving the salmon salad, strawberries and cheese and biscuits which had been intended for consumption on the plane. It was 1.30 am when we finally left. This time we managed to pass through the various checks at Moscow airport in just over an hour . . . but it was 4.30 am and the place was deserted!

There was a funny moment when the customs people asked

me why I was leaving with more money than I had taken into the country two day earlier. Before you enter the USSR you have to fill in a form detailing all your cash, travellers' cheques and valuables. On leaving you have to fill in another form saying how much you have left.

'I won it playing cards,' I said. I don't think the man understood but further hold-ups were avoided when his colleague nodded his head and smiled. We landed at Stansted at 7 am English time after a sleepless night. John Lyall's fears that the journey may have taken a lot out of us physically and mentally were realised the following Saturday when we struggled to draw 1-1 at home against Oldham. I don't think I have ever been so tired as I was at the end of that eventful week!

16

The Hard Games

Football is not all about glamour and big crowds. Many matches I have played in, particularly in the Second Division with West Ham, have been 'bread and butter matches', games against uncompromising opponents who want to stop you playing.

Such a game was the West Ham v Sheffield Wednesday League game at Upton Park on 6 December 1980. I have selected this game as a typical example to show what I do in a game and how I react to this different kind of challenge. It was, I recall, not one of my better days, especially as I made headlines the next day for being cautioned for what the referee called 'a vicious tackle from behind'. West Ham were on top of the Second Division at the time and Wednesday were fourth with a goal tally of twenty-six goals for and twenty-three against from twenty matches, which was an indication of how they were playing. Ernie Gregory, the former West Ham player who played a record 383 League games as a goalkeeper for the club, had watched Wednesday and warned us they would play an offside game. He was right about that. Wednesday's back line of defenders closed up quickly behind the play and David Cross and Paul Goddard were caught out a few times. Crowds do not like to see the offside game and you cannot blame them.

Ernie, who assists with general administration and coaching at the club, also said Wednesday would use a long ball game, playing the ball deep into the corners for Andy McCulloch and Terry Curran, their front pair, to chase. In the second half in particular, Wednesday used that system well and caused us a lot of problems by missing out the midfield. Curran, who used to be in the First Division with Southampton, is a particularly skilful player and soon showed that the ball could be played up to him without his defenders having to worry about it coming straight back. His control is good. McCulloch also impressed me as being a much improved player from his early days playing for a number of London clubs.

Jack Charlton, the Wednesday manager, had decided to use Jeff Johnson, the twenty-seven-year-old Welshman who was at Crystal Palace in Malcolm Allison's first spell there, as my personal marker. This often happens in matches, particularly in the lower divisions where the opposing team is prepared to take one of its players out of the game to look after me exclusively. When I look at the fixture list and see what the next few matches are, I know at once who will get the job. Steve Powell did it when we played Derby County. He is a sound and disciplined player and so is Neil Robinson of Swansea City. But the player who has done the task better than anyone in my experience is the relatively unknown Gordon Coleman of Preston North End, a lad from Nottingham who has played more than 200 League games. Whenever we have played Preston, he has never been a yard from me. I cannot say I have enjoyed playing in matches when I have been shadowed so effectively but I guess the other fellow is not enjoying it much either. In Italy this oppressive close marking goes on in every match and is one reason why I would not like to play there.

I make it a policy never to talk to my marker. Some players such as Stan Bowles will sometimes have a go and say things like 'You're not going to get near me today', but I believe silence is the best course of action. If you start goading opponents they are likely to try and take it out on you. If you are playing badly and you start to show your frustration by complaining, that will give them more confidence. A long time ago I decided that just getting on with the game and leaving the verbals to the others was the right way of going about it.

The match against Wednesday was played on a windy and blustery day. In cricket the experts are always talking about the conditions – what the pitch is doing, how the atmosphere is helping the bowlers swing the ball and what effect the sun will have later on when the spin bowlers are brought on. In football the conditions are hardly ever taken into account unless the pitch is frozen or is very muddy. A still day and a soft and yielding pitch provide the best conditions. The attacking player always has a better chance when the ground is a little muddy on top. Most of my 'training' as a boy was on the mud at 'The Field' and it has served me well ever since. The worst possible condition in my view is when there is a strong wind. As a touch player, I find I have to keep adjusting, and it makes playing very difficult. I can be shaping up to control the ball with my right foot only to find it has veered away at the last moment towards my left side and I have to adjust accordingly. The wind also makes it harder to find the target with longer-range passes. If you are kicking with the wind, the 'weight' of the pass has to be altered slightly and vice versa if you are kicking against it. In the first half eight of my twenty-three passes were twenty yards or more. Two went astray. In the second half, when conditions were less favourable, five of the twenty passes I made failed to reach the target.

I made six headers in the game which is well above average for me. It has often been said that my heading for someone of my height is not good enough and that is a view I have always shared. Since heading the only goal in the 1980 FA Cup Final, I seemed to have had more success in the air, chiefly because I find myself getting into the box more to meet crosses.

West Ham's first goal against Wednesday, in the thirty-ninth minute, came when I headed in from close range, a similar effort to my Wembley goal. That equalized Ante Mirocevic's goal in the thirty-fourth minute, a far-post header against the run of the play. Pat Holland scored the second two minutes later but that was the end of the scoring. We had to fight hard in the second half to hold on to that 2-1 lead.

There was an incident in the fifty-sixth minute which showed just how much luck plays a part in professional football. Paul Goddard put me into the six-yard box on the left-hand side and as their goalkeeper Bob Bolder came out, I thought I had flicked the ball round him but he must have got a hand to it because it did not finish up in the back of the net. The 30,476 crowd must have been surprised as I failed to realize that the ball had in fact trickled along behind me as I continued to run and all I had to do was turn and tap it in. But instead of looking to where the ball was, on my right, I looked to the left and in that split second a defender came clattering in to knock it away.

Getting into the box more has meant I now have more goal-scoring opportunities and my record in the 1980-81 season was an improvement on previous years. Up to then my League record was 64 goals in 397 appearances, or one goal in every six matches. Martin Peters' record was one goal in every 3½ matches which shows what a midfield player can do if he is a good finisher. Heading and goal-scoring are areas where I felt I could have done more in my career.

I made three tackles during the ninety minutes of the match against Wednesday which is about my normal quota. I am not a great tackler although I have tried to be more aggressive. I made eight runs with the ball; some were productive, while others came to nothing. There are some clubs where running with the ball is discouraged. The philosophy is 'give it and go'. But I believe if there is a chance to take defenders on and put them out of the game it is worth taking. With Alan Devonshire doing the same thing on the left side of the field, this gives West Ham many more attacking options than most sides.

I take a lot of the free kicks, particularly ones away from the penalty area. There were four in the Wednesday match and I tried to bend them into the box for David Cross or Alvin Martin to get a header in. When you take a free kick or a penalty, you automatically turn to your stronger leg which is why I usually take free kicks with my right foot which was my stronger leg when I was a small boy.

I committed one foul in the match and it led to me being cautioned. I do not think it was so much because of that foul, rather it was a follow-on of an earlier incident. As Alan Devonshire was going through, Jeff Johnson blatantly handled, or so I thought, but the referee, David Letts, a police sergeant from Hampshire, waved play on. I said: 'Ref, how about the hand ball?' He replied: 'I didn't see anything.' And I countered: 'You must have been the only person in the ground who didn't see it.'

I never talk to referees normally and I immediately regretted having said it. I could see that the referee was displeased.

Later, when Wednesday had a spell of pressure one of their players came up behind me near our penalty area and as I tried to stick a foot out to knock the ball away brought him down. The referee then said: 'I am going to book you.' I said 'What for?' 'For a vicious tackle from behind,' he replied. We had to laugh about it afterwards. John Lyall remarked : 'You've let us in for it now.' Earlier that week the Football Association had issued their charter about hooliganism and the behaviour of players on the pitch. John was quoted in one of the morning papers that he would see that West Ham's players behaved responsibly and set an example to the spectators.

Though the caution had a farcical element because my 'tackle' could never be termed 'vicious' it had been my own fault. I should never have spoken to the referee over the hand-ball incident. In fact, I hardly ever speak to referees. This is not because I have any bad feeling for them. If I was asked to name some out of the eighty or so on the Football League list I would struggle to reach five. I believe they are there to do a difficult job and should be left to do it without players chipping in with advice. Dissent has now become one of the prime offences and it is foolish for players to argue. Few referees will change a decision because a player has said something to them. More likely they will get out their book.

Billy Bonds was cautioned a couple of minutes after I was shown the yellow card following what I thought was an innocent tackle. I was nearby and all I heard him say was 'Oh, no', but that must have been construed as dissent. There are a number of referees who do not accept chat from players so my general rule is not to talk to any of them.

Many people have suggested that referees should become full-time professionals in order to improve efficiency. Another suggestion is the introduction of ex-players into refereeing where their experience would be of great benefit. I am not sure that either of these is the answer. Certainly, a series of meetings between referees and ex-players would benefit the former from the point of view of finding out what factors particularly frustrate the players. It would give them a valuable insight into players' thoughts and help them in their interpretation of the laws. One example is 'advantage' which some whistle-happy referees never give time to develop. My final comment on refereeing is that I would like to see the compulsory retirement age of forty-eight applied with a little more flexibility as a number of top-quality referees who were still very fit and capable have been lost to the game.

One of the more imaginative proposals accepted by the chairmen at the meeting at Solihull in 1981 was the one making it compulsory for apprentices to learn the laws of the game. Experienced players who have taken FA Coaching courses know the laws because a paper on laws is part of the course, but there are many players who are not conversant with every facet of every law and this sometimes causes trouble on the pitch.

I am often asked why footballers do not accept decisions the way rugby players accept them. There is hardly any dissent in rugby which is a more physical game. I suppose tradition has a lot to do with it. In rugby the tradition is to get on with the game. In soccer a tradition has grown up in post-war years to moan and complain if a decision goes against you. Another factor is that in a rugby scrum it is difficult to see who has fouled who whereas in soccer it is a one against one situation.

I did not see Jack Charlton, the Wednesday manager, after the match. His team had played the way I had expected them to play and it had been one of our toughest matches. 'We've given them a fright,' he was quoted as saying. All of Charlton's sides are well organized and hard to break down. Middlesbrough were the same when he was there. Jack is different from most managers because football is not the sum total of his life. With many of them it is a compulsion that occupies all their waking hours. But Jack has an interesting and varied life away from the game. After training, he will disappear to go shooting or fishing and delegate responsibility to other people. Not many managers are big enough to do that. I believe that was one of the reasons he declined the Chelsea managership in 1981 as these relaxing breaks would have been impossible in London!

17

Injury

Just before half time in the match against Newcastle United at Upton Park on 24 March 1979, I lost possession of the ball near the edge of the Newcastle penalty area, chased back and retrieved it, and as I laid the ball to a colleague, a Newcastle player tackled me. I went over so awkwardly, with my right foot bent back under my leg that I feared I had broken my ankle. Except for a chipped bone in an ankle, a back injury, a broken nose and various slight strains and pulls, I have never been seriously injured.

In the few seconds you are lying on the ground in agony your first thoughts are always pessimistic. It hurt so much it could not be a sprain. Rob Jenkins, our trainer, arrived with his bag and as he took off my tie up to examine the foot, said: 'What happened?' The trainer will always say that even if it is right in front of the dug out and he has had a perfect view. The player could have been whacked on the thigh and as he fell twisted an ankle, so it is the ankle that needs treatment, not the thigh. The player has always to be the guide.

I could not put any weight on my foot and had to be helped off. We were 4-0 up at the time and playing as well as at any time that year. It was our first season in the Second Division after a twenty-year spell in the First and we were fifth in the table with twelve not too hard matches left. To my annoyance I did not recover from injury until the last game, and we ended up in fifth place. I played only twenty-one matches that season. I missed six games in November and December when I twisted the other ankle in training. I went up to head the ball with a young American who was training with us and he nudged me slightly, just enough to put me off balance and I went over on my left ankle. However, the Newcastle injury was the worst – it turned out to be severe damage to the ligaments at the front of the ankle, not a break – and for a whole month the swelling would not go down, despite every kind of treatment. With ligament injuries there is no way of telling how long they will take to heal. Frequently the damage has long-term effects and the joint is never as sound again. Often this results in arthritis in old age. As you sit on the treatment table for hour after hour every day, you wonder what effect your injury will have on your career. This fear of an abrupt end to your footballing life may explain why the soccer player is more demanding than the average working man. He wants to make as much money out of it as he can, while he can. He knows it could end in one tackle as it did for Geoff Nulty, the former Newcastle player who went to Everton and badly damaged his knee in a collision with Liverpool's Jimmy Case.

Mick McGiven, West Ham's reserve team coach, had to endure a broken leg and cartilage operations on his knee. Ultimately his career was ended prematurely by the knee injury. John Lyall's career was also shattered by a knee injury at the age of twenty-three. The dread of injury should not be underplayed. Given that West Ham is probably fairly typical, a professional footballer has a thirty per cent chance of being seriously injured. At one time, out of sixteen players in the squad, four had had cartilage operations (Phil Parkes, McGiven, Pat Holland and Stuart Pearson, who has had three operations on his knee) and three, Frank Lampard, McGiven and Holland, had broken legs. That is five players badly hurt out of sixteen. The others including Paul Brush, Alvin Martin, Ray Stewart, Billy Bonds, Geoff Pike, Bobby Ferguson, Alan Devonshire, Paul Allen, David Cross and myself had all been injured at various times but not too seriously. Geoff Hurst had his career ended by a back injury and Ron Boyce, the youth team coach, was similarly affected. 'Ticker' had disc trouble. Joe Royle and Dave Watson are still playing after having discs removed from their backs. John McDowell, now with Norwich, had knee trouble and his knee has never really recovered.

The list of players who have had to quit is a long one – Colin Bell, Tony Green, Mick Jones and Malcolm Macdonald among them. Others are still playing with knee trouble, including Charlie George, Andy Gray, Keith Weller, Gordon Hill, Tony Currie, Bruce Rioch, Alex Cropley and Kevin Beattie. Kevin's case is probably the most tragic of them all. When he first came in to the England side he was hailed as the new Duncan Edwards and he had all the assets to become such a player. But four operations on his knee never gave him a chance. After a hard game or a sustained period of training, his knee will swell up again and he has to rest. He is still playing for Ipswich, but not too often.

With the inevitable smaller staffs that are soon to be forced on clubs by economic circumstances, the risk of players having to go out and play when not fit will be increased. The pressure to play is there anyway, from within. Not many players enjoy lazing around having treatment. They would rather be playing. And some of them want to take a chance of playing because they will lose their bonuses. To my knowledge, there are not many who feign injury. There are, however, players who can be convinced by the manager that it will be all right to play in an important match. When I was younger I would turn out when I felt less than fully fit. Nowadays, experience has taught me that it is better to overestimate rather than underestimate the time needed to recover. I like to add a week on just to make sure. It is pointless coming back ninety per cent fit, breaking down and being out twice as long.

Kevin Keegan's burning desire to give Southampton value for money let him down in his first season back in England. He tried to come back too soon after a hamstring injury and had to go away and rest completely. Kevin is a player who loves football and wants to play. It is hard to hold him back. But there is little point in risking a hamstring strain. You think it is better then it goes again. You cannot ease your way back with such an injury; it has to be absolutely right before you can play in a match.

There are players who in their rush to return to action after injury will ask for a pain-killing injection. I am not one of them and I do not recommend it to any player, at any level of the game. A local anaesthetic can deaden the warning signals and more harm can be done unwittingly. The only time I had a painkiller was when I bruised an instep and it was painful when I kicked the ball. That, I feel, is permissible. For muscle strains to have this treatment is asking for trouble. The player should always have the last say in these matters.

Although I do not like injections, it was a couple of jabs from England doctor Vernon Edwards which 'cured' my ankle after the Newcastle injury. Before the start of the Home Championship at the end of the season I was still being troubled by the injury, but Ron Greenwood included me in the squad. 'We're well covered in midfield, just come along for the ride,' he said. I had played a reserve game on a hard pitch and the foot was still sore. Vernon Edwards gave me some tablets and asked if I minded having two injections, one on either side of the foot. At that stage in the season it did not matter and I went ahead and had them. The fluid disappeared almost overnight and next day Ron selected me as a substitute for the match against Wales and I came on for Ray Wilkins. Three days later I played in the 3-1 victory over Scotland.

I have had three cortisone injections at various times when suffering from groin strains, but I am not keen on cortisone. I believe there is a risk of long-term side effects. It is difficult for a player to take a stand over this. He is an employee of the club and if he is told to have one, he needs to be strong minded to refuse.

The spray which is used by the trainer when he comes on to the field is a different matter. I see no harm when a bruise or a knock is sprayed by a local anaesthetic. But I wouldn't want it done in the case of muscle strain.

Since injuring both ankles I now have them strapped before matches and I also take no chances during training. I use the Elastoplast sticky type of bandage which holds its position unlike crepe bandages which tend to slip. These bandages not only support the ankle they safeguard against minor cuts and abrasions. Most players strap their ankles. It is rare that an experienced player has managed to survive without suffering ankle strains which might have left him with weakened ligaments. Alan Devonshire wears a special ankle protector and feels he needs it. I have always worn shin guards myself and I agree with him that the ankle also needs protection. Several players, including Paul Mariner, wear a specially designed shin guard which furthermore protects the ankle all the way round the foot. It reduces the risk of being injured by tackles from behind and is a sensible precaution for players who play mainly with their back to goal.

Players with ankle trouble do not like playing on hard, bumpy pitches and until recently West Ham's Upton Park was a pitch which could cause problems. As the season neared its close, we used to have a spot the grass contest among ourselves. But since the introduction of a new sprinkler system and improved drainage, there is now far more grass on the pitch and it is less bumpy.

One injury you cannot beat is back trouble. When I was nineteen, I woke one morning with a sore back and unwisely played in a reserve game. It was so bad I had to come off after ten minutes. The trainer put me in a hot bath and when I came out, I could not move. I had to be driven home, crouching on all fours on the back seat of my father's car. The pain was unbearable and it was some time before I was fit again. Since then, I have always slept with a board under my mattress and fortunately the trouble has not recurred.

Not long after this in a game against Luton I went up to head the ball in the goal area and in my effort to keep it down drove my face into the back of a defender's head. It left me with a depressed fracture of the nose which had to be pulled back into place in hospital by a suction device.

As a player who twists and turns a lot, I could have had a lot of problems with my knees but fortunately I have escaped. That is my good luck. The knee is the most intricate joint in the body and once you start having trouble with it, that's the beginning of the end as so many players have found. I have been very lucky in my years in the game: so many other players have not.

18

Grounds

After the 1980 Charity Shield when his team beat West Ham 1-0 in a somewhat lifeless match, Liverpool manager Bob Paisley attacked the state of the Wembley pitch, claiming that the grass was too long. 'I thought it was specially prepared for the West Indies fast bowlers,' he said. 'There was too much grass left on which took the pace off the ball and made it very hard work for the players.'

There were some things that could be criticized at Wembley that day but the pitch was not one of them. I thought the pitch played well in that match, as it usually does. The main difference between playing on a normal League pitch and the Wembley pitch is that when you go out at Wembley you know that the playing surface will be lush and true. It is maintained to a very high standard and it is one of my favourite pitches.

There are certain conditions, however, when it is a disadvantage to be playing at Wembley. When it is wet, the tightly knit grass tends to come out in divots and players lose their footing more easily than on a League pitch. This explains why so many England players appear to be wearing the wrong footwear on certain occasions. It is nothing to do with their boots. It is the grass that is the trouble. I find I need a larger stud than normal in these conditions. Even on dry days at Wembley I wear a reasonably long stud because invariably the pitch retains moisture after watering. If I used rubber studs I would never keep my feet. When Wembley is wet I find it can detrimentally affect my game, mainly when I am trying for longish through passes over the top of defenders. The ball can skid through more quickly than anticipated and instead of being correctly weighted, the pass overshoots the target. An example of a match where England's performance was affected by the conditions was the friendly against Spain in March 1981. Trevor Francis, in particular, found it hazardous to twist and turn on the slippery surface and consequently he had one of his least effective games.

But the worst playing surface I can remember at Wembley was the frozen pitch which greeted us for a friendly against Czechoslovakia in 1978. The match came close to being called off and after our 1-0 victory, everyone said how well the Czechs had kept their feet. Whereas most of our players wore short nylon studs or rubber boots with suction holes, the Czechs wore an Adidas snow boot the soles of which were covered with pimpled rubber like a magnified impression of an old fashioned table tennis bat. West Ham obtained some of these boots shortly afterwards and used them in a 4-0 victory over Orient in similar conditions.

Wembley used to have some of the biggest dressing rooms in the game. Since the Don Revie era these have been restyled and made smaller. When outsiders come in as they often do – officials, club representatives, attendants and so on – there is very little space to move around. Instead of pegs to hang up clothes, there are now lockers. Wembley is the only ground in the country that has these American style lockers. I am not sure they are a good idea. Most players prefer what they are used to at their own clubs – pegs. But Wembley still leads in its washing facilities. The plunge baths are the biggest and there are also six individual baths. Despite there being showers very few players take one after a game. They like to soak in the bath. The showers are more often used before a game. Ray Stewart and Geoff Pike always like a cold shower before a game. They believe it sharpens them up. England's Ray Wilkins also has a shower beforehand.

No experience open to a professional footballer quite matches the roar from the crowd when he steps out of the Wembley tunnel. I have experienced the Wembley roar a few times now and it still brings a tingle inside me. Even Anfield cannot match it. Apart from Upton Park and Wembley, Anfield and Old Trafford are my two favourite grounds. Both of these grounds have usually been full when I have played there and the atmosphere is unequalled at any other League ground.

The Anfield crowd is one of the most knowledgeable in football and will always applaud good things from the opposing team. I suppose they can afford to because Liverpool hardly ever lose at home so there is little to upset them. I have never been on the winning side at Anfield. One year we led 1-0 and 2-1, but we eventually went down 2-3, a trifle unluckily.

The Liverpool dressing rooms are spacious and, as you would expect, well appointed. Surprisingly, Old Trafford's dressing rooms are not as impressive as you would imagine. They are adequate, no more. As the coach draws up outside the ground, you are conscious that here is a great club. Thousands of people are milling about outside or making their way to the imposing stands which now ring the pitch. The club shop is packed with supporters. Maine Road is similarly imposing although it lacks the tradition and support of Old Trafford. One of my favourite grounds is Elland Road, Leeds, especially after West Ham's FA Cup semi-final success there against Everton in 1980. The pitch is one of the best in the League and is also one of the largest, being 117 by 76 yards compared with West Ham's at 110 × 72 yards. I prefer playing on a bigger pitch as it is easier to get away from defenders. A small pitch cramps my style.

The facilities at Elland Road off the pitch are inferior to those at many First Division grounds, which I find surprising. There is no toilet in each of the dressing rooms and the players have to share one about twenty yards away. This can be embarrassing especially as there are players who visit the toilet a number of times before games.

Arsenal's Highbury is a ground which has not been re-developed significantly, but is still one of the best appointed grounds in the League. No other club has such an impressive marble entrance, or marble, heated floors in the dressing rooms. I have been impressed with the improvements made at Coventry City's Highfield Road in recent years. Highfield Road is now one of the most modern grounds in the country and boasts possibly the finest training facilities. They are following the Ipswich example of concentrating on home-produced players and making the club viable by managing sensibly their resources. Coventry will never match Aston Villa or Birmingham City in gate potential and have sought to earn money by other means.

Building new stands is not always the best way of maximizing income as Nottingham Forest, Wolves and Newcastle have discovered. QPR chairman Jim Gregory has done it gradually at Loftus Road but his club has never been able to attract consistently high attendances. Chelsea, their close rivals, used to be one of the League's best supported clubs until they went into the Second Division and were almost crippled by the financial burdens of their new stand.

Chelsea are one of a number of clubs whose home dressing room is bigger and more comfortable than the away team's dressing room. Brian Clough once said it needed a coat of paint and since then no one has ever complained about the state of decoration. It is an oddly-shaped room at Stamford Bridge for the visitors – long and narrow. Tottenham Hotspur have followed them in the business of stand rebuilding and their players have had to endure the inconvenience of having to change in a Portakabin in the car park. Since having their stand damaged in a fire, Bristol Rovers have also had to change in makeshift accommodation.

Spurs used to have one of the worst pitches in the League. Now it is one of the best, capable of taking an enormous amount of rainwater without flooding. The standard of pitches in this country has improved dramatically in recent years. This is because most grounds have installed new drainage and underground sprinkler systems which effectively waters the whole pitch and protects the grass. Earlier in my career, Upton Park used to be almost bare by the end of the season with only small triangles on the corners covered in grass. Half the pitches in the League were the same and players used to dislike having to play end of season matches on these dusty surfaces. But now pitches remain well grassed right through to the end of the season and there is less opportunity to blame the conditions for a poor performance. Ipswich used to possess the most envied playing surface in the League and though Portman Road remains a good pitch to play on, a number of other clubs now have pitches of equal quality. Middlesbrough, for example, have a well-grassed, well-drained surface.

The pitch at Upton Park has been greatly improved and the facilities are now among the best in the country. Each dressing room has claret and blue tiling with strips of rubber flooring for players to warm up on before going out onto the field. Most players like to do some exercises in the dressing room and if the floor is slippery they can injure themselves.

I am not in favour of playing on artificial surfaces and I regret that the Football League gave permission to QPR to construct one at Loftus Road. The game is at its most attractive when played on varying, natural surfaces. On a true surface, such as Astroturf and Omniturf, it will be harder for attacking players to take advantage of mistakes by defenders. The ball will be in the air more and I am sure there will be fewer goals. Ultimately, the game would become less of a spectacle as it is in North America where they have to jazz it up to keep the interest of the fans. There is also the risk of permanent injury to players' joints caused by playing on an unyielding surface. If sides played on artificial pitches in the wholehearted manner they do now, half of them would come off the field at the end with friction burns on their skin.

I am also opposed to ground-sharing which was to have been pioneered in this country by Wimbledon and Crystal Palace but was subsequently abandoned. It is a short cut towards one club losing its identity and being forced to live in the shadow of another. It may have economic advantages but I can think of few footballing ones.

If one of the clubs starts doing well while the other one fades, there is a danger that its fans will switch their allegiance and the first club could become the reserve side or nursery. The tradition in English football is that each area should have its own club and should be followed by a hard core of supporters and I feel it is bad for the game if this pattern is broken up. I cannot imagine West Ham fans being in favour of, say, sharing a ground with Orient or Charlton. And even in a city such as Sheffield which boasts two teams with First Division quality grounds, I doubt whether the idea of ground sharing would be popular with the respective sets of supporters.

Ground sharing takes place in Italy, West Germany and some

South American countries because the grounds are municipally owned and the clubs cannot afford to build their own stadium of similar size. But in this country there are no major stadiums owned by councils. They would have to be built out of the rates or taxes and in the present economic recession that seems unrealistic.

My trips to Second Division grounds in the past two years have convinced me that there are not many clubs whose grounds are worthy of First Division status. And there is scant prospect of that changing because money is needed to spend on the team ahead of ground facilities.

The biggest and noisiest ground I have been to is the Maracana Stadium in Rio de Janeiro, Brazil. I was injured at the time and sat on the bench. The noise from the incessant drumming was still throbbing through my head hours later. The Munich stadium is probably the most modern and efficent I have played in. It is municipally owned and was designed for the 1976 Olympics. There is no comparable stadium anywhere in Britain. Hampden Park is nearing the end of its life, but remains an exciting place for a visiting player with an atmosphere rivalling Wembley's. For international matches, the Scottish FA may, however, eventually use the redeveloped Ibrox Stadium which is close to being all-seat.

At all these grounds I have managed to be the last player out onto the pitch. I cannot remember how this started, but it is a tradition at West Ham and I have found with England that as no one wants the position I can still go out last. Like most players, I am quite superstitious. If we get a couple of good results when I am wearing a particular jacket or suit, I will keep wearing that suit in the hope that it will continue to bring success.

In our 1980 FA Cup run, David Cross was sent a small medallion by a supporter and wore it all the way to Wembley. Players often receive such gifts from fans. Don Revie was one of the most superstitious people in football. I know of hardly any players or managers who do not look for omens to help them. Success in football is to a certain extent dependent on luck and it seems natural to try and court it. I cannot recall a single player who openly ridicules the superstitious habits of his colleagues.

Hooliganism is the main reason why family audiences are

disappearing from our game and until there are changes in the community and in school life I cannot see the position changing much. The unruliness at grounds has led to most clubs putting up fences which is extremely sad. I would not want to watch a game through such a screen.

The clubs have decided that prevention is better than cure and the innocent suffer with the guilty. Miraculously, West Ham have been able to avoid installing fencing. Before each game the club announcer reminds the fans not to spoil the club's record by running on to the pitch. There has been one serious invasion when Manchester United, a club whose reputation has suffered at times, were the visitors but the directors felt it did not warrant building fences. I hope that continues. It will be a black day in the club's history if our fans have to be caged in.

I would love to see family audiences here as there are in America. However, having visited grounds in Fort Lauderdale and Los Angeles I can see reasons why this may be difficult to attain. The North American Soccer League season is played in hot, mainly dry weather and the fans sit out in the open. Very few stadiums are covered as they are here. Our climate would not allow this to happen. The standard of living is also higher in America and blue collar workers can afford to take their families to sporting events. Car parking is much easier and cheaper, and fast foods and drinks are more readily obtainable. Consequently there is more incentive to go to a match when the weather is warm enough to be able to wear a T-shirt and you can have drink brought to your seat in paper cups. American audiences are much better behaved than ours and there is practically no hooliganism. Crowds are also more patriotic. They do not boo, or sing something else during the playing of the National Anthem as has happened at Wembley.

In the last decade Football League clubs have started to take steps to improve facilities sufficiently to persuade parents to take their children to matches. More and more clubs have family sections with reduced prices. I hope the trend continues.

The critics are right when they say that the poor standard of grounds is a factor in declining attendances. Most of the grounds I visit have not changed in my time in football – except for a new coat of paint. But there are historical and financial reasons why there are no new, all-seated stadiums in this country as there are in most other countries. A lot of grounds here were built around the turn of the century before the arrival of the car and have little or no parking space. It is easy to suggest that these grounds should be sold and new ones built on the outskirts of cities but no club in the country has the capital to do that. So the old grounds have to be patched up in the absence of municipally owned stadiums. Millions of pounds were spent before the Safety of Sports Grounds Act was brought in and since then millions more have been devoted to making grounds safer.

Clubs are naturally frightened to commit themselves to a big outlay because, as Chelsea found, an ambitious redevelopment can be financially crippling, almost fatal. Clubs like Nottingham Forest and Wolves have only been able to build new stands after they were promoted from the Second Division. If the Corporation Tax position was altered and clubs were allowed to offset spending on grounds against tax, there would be a dramatic improvement in facilities at most grounds. The FA have campaigned for this change without success for many years.

Although some of our grounds are unsatisfactory, it should be acknowledged that many clubs have made the effort to rebuild. Almost half the First Division clubs, for instance, have built new stands, including Ipswich, Aston Villa, Tottenham, Nottingham Forest, Manchester United, Leeds, Coventry, Wolves, Leicester City and Crystal Palace. About a third of the Second Division clubs also have new stands.

Viewing at most English grounds is in fact reasonably good. Fans are not stuck high up at the back of open concrete stands with a running track between them and the playing pitch. English grounds are much more intimate and there is more atmosphere than at most Continental grounds. Few grounds anywhere else in the world allow the spectators to be as close to the action as fans are at Upton Park.

19

The Future

As I passed my thirty-third birthday in October 1981, people are invariably asking me about my future. My contract with West Ham ends in the summer of 1983 and at this stage I doubt whether I shall continue to play after that. I have already indicated here that I cannot see soccer management as an ideal job for me, mainly because of the insecurity.

I would envisage my connections with football being continued more with schoolboy coaching, such as the Eurosports Village project. Some people have suggested that I might undertake more work in television. I have enjoyed the times I have been asked to appear on television, usually as a panelist at big matches, but it is a difficult field to break into and that is not going to change much, even with the introduction of a fourth channel.

I remember Bob Wilson making me laugh when he related a story about his first appearance on television. He had just been sent to watch Arsenal play Manchester United at Highbury and left before the end to race back to Shepherd's Bush to deliver his report on 'Grandstand'. In the taxi he kept practising his introduction: 'I've just returned from Highbury where Alan Ball has starred in Arsenal's 2-0 defeat of League leaders Manchester United.' Having repeated it over and over in his mind, he sat anxiously waiting for his cue from Frank Bough. At last his moment arrived and Frank said: 'And now here's Bob Wilson who has just returned from Highbury where I believe Alan Ball starred in Arsenal's 2-0 defeat of League leaders Manchester United.'

Although momentarily stunned by Frank having stolen his

opening line, Bob managed to stagger through and now he is established as an important member of the team.

Another alternative at the end of my playing career, is to concentrate more fully on my business involvements. Early in 1981, Sports International, one of the four companies I am involved with, signed a contract with some American businessmen to develop 670 acres of land in Ocala, North Florida. When completed, the site will have an 18-hole championship golf course which will be called 'Blue Chip' with each hole a replica of well-known holes at the world's most famous courses and also a second 18-hole course called 'Golden Greens'. In addition there will be three hundred and fifty luxury apartments and a second phase will include a number of villas with half-acre plots. There is a theatre at the existing site, which was a school, and it is intended to turn that into a convention centre.

Work on the first phase, which is developing fifty acres, has already started. It is the most exciting venture I have ever been associated with but it is unlikely that I will live permanently in America: my roots are too firmly bedded here. But if the development emerges as anticipated I can see myself spending half the year in Florida and the other half here. Whether such a move might mean I would be available to play for an American club is not clear at the moment, but it is certainly a possibility.

The proposed site is in an area of natural beauty, mainly woodland, sixty miles from Disney World in Orlando. It is within thirty miles of a beach on the Gulf of Mexico side and Daytona Beach is less than an hour's drive away on the Atlantic coast of Florida. The golf courses are being designed by Ron Garl, a recognized expert, and the 'Blue Chip' course promises to be one of the most interesting courses in the world.

I am a keen golfer myself (handicap 18) and used to play a lot with Bryan Robson when he was at West Ham. His handicap was three and he is a former winner of the professional footballers' annual golfing event. I am a member of Chigwell Golf Club and try to play as often as I can.

Sports International was founded in 1979 by my business manager and friend Walter Howe to sponsor young golfers. We are currently sponsoring four English players in Disney World and have a management interest with six US players on the PGA circuit.

The opportunities at Ocala International are limitless. The area is famed for horse breeding and riding will be one of the features of the project. There will also be swimming pools, tennis courts and opportunities for playing and coaching soccer. In short, it will be a sporting paradise.

Apart from Sports International I am a director of three other companies that are unconnected with sport. The longest standing directorship is with Colbrook Plastics, a small firm in Stratford which I set up with a friend, Colin McGowan, manufacturing plastic comb binders and slide binders used in the book binding trade. It is ticking over well despite the recession with a turnover of between £250,000 and £300,000 a year and twelve employees. I do all the book-keeping and accounts and Hilkka helps with the secretarial work.

Another good friend, Len Edwards, formed his own company, Leabrook Contracts, of which I am a director. This company is involved with demolition and commodity trading in iron and steel and my main contribution is on the public relations side.

My final business involvement is with Malvern Construction which is run by Walter Howe. Although many building companies had a bad time in recent years, Malvern has done well. It specializes in refurbishing council houses while the tenants are still in occupation. With most local authorities unable to build new houses because of spending cuts, many councils spend more of their housing allocation on renewing older properties. The advantage of this system is that they do not have to rehouse the occupants while the work is going on. Rents are frozen until the work is finished.

Most evenings I will have some book-keeping or paper work to do in my study at my Shenfield home after playing with the children. Collette, who was born in January 1975, is similar to me in personality. She is very quiet and studious, but has also inherited my weakness of being rather untidy. I have always been a bit of a casual type of person and can be too lethargic if I am not careful. If I have nothing to do I am liable to slump into a chair and relax. That kind of attitude can spill over on to the football pitch. I have problems, for instance, when I am on tour with England. There is not a lot to do after morning training and I can find myself becoming bored. It can make me sluggish mentally when it comes to playing a match. I operate much better when I have plenty to occupy me and thrive on a busy life.

Warren, who was born in July 1978, is like Hilkka – lively and orderly. Running a business, or several businesses, from my home as well as putting in time at the offices means I rarely have a chance to take it easy which is a good thing. Hilkka is terrific. She has a very good business sense, having been a hotel receptionist and then worked on the sales side. She keeps my diary and is in charge of the files. As I am away so much on football trips she has almost as much to do with the plastics company as I do.

Since the arrival of Phil Parkes, Paul Goddard and Alan Devonshire, who live to the west of London and travel a long distance, West Ham have started training later. We used to start at ten o'clock but it is now ten-thirty which means I can usually put in a few business calls before I leave home. But doing two jobs – football and my business activities – means that I have to socialise a lot and I have to watch my weight. I don't eat potatoes or sweets because I put on weight easily. My best weight is about thirteen stone five pounds but I can quickly shoot up to thirteen ten or twelve if I don't watch myself. I am just over six foot six in height and slightly on the heavy side for a footballer.

Despite all the socialising, I do not drink which I suppose makes me an exception in football circles. I have always drunk Coke and other soft drinks. People cannot accept that I do not drink simply because I do not like alcohol. They suspect there must be some deeper reason or that I was brought up in a teetotal house which was not the case. Both my mother and father drank occasionally in moderation and my brother and I were never discouraged from drinking. It is just that I do not like the taste of alcohol. In my early days in the game I was constantly ribbed about my abstinence because most football people are drinkers. The other players were always trying to slip spirits into my glass of Coke but I was rarely caught out. These days they have given up because everyone knows I am not a drinker and can spot a mickey finn even in the dimmest of bars!

I am not a moraliser about other people's habits. If people want to drink it is up to them but football is such a disciplined life that I feel it is unwise to break the unwritten rules too near a match. I was at Blackpool in 1971 at the start of the year when four West Ham players were disciplined by Ron Greenwood for drinking after hours. At the time I was a member of the squad and not in the first team and like most of the others I did not know about it until the following week when the story broke in the newspapers.

Probably nothing more would have been heard about it if West Ham had not lost 0-4 in a third round FA Cup tie on an ice rink of a pitch at Bloomfield Road some hours later. Blackpool were relegated that season with only twenty-three points and, although we just escaped relegation ourselves, it was a surprise result. As we were so low in the table, it virtually meant the end of our season.

Despite the Blackpool affair, I would not say that West Ham has been renowned as a club of drinkers. The opportunities are always there for players to have a night out and be fêted but we have a very responsible bunch of players. I always smile when I hear stories to the effect that so-and-so player has been seen out drinking. Tony, my brother, has told me on several occasions how people have come up to him and said they have seen me drinking in a pub with him before matches. They do not know he is a teetotaller like me and neither of us goes into pubs!

There was one particularly amusing story concerning drinking, but that involved my father-in-law from Finland. He came over to stay with us and the day he arrived I was due to play an evening League fixture at Upton Park. Before we all left home to go to the match he decided to stretch his legs after the journey, but unfortunately he had not returned when it was time for us to go. It was a little worrying as he did not speak a word of English, but Hilkka thought he would be all right.

Later, just as I was leaving Upton Park after the game, a policeman arrived asking me to go to Barkingside police station. Hilkka and I rushed to the station where we found her father quietly drinking tea in a detention room. Apparently during his walk he had wandered into our local public house where he had sampled some English beer. Finding himself locked out when he returned home, he proceeded to act strangely enough to attract the attention of a neighbour who called in the local police. Fortunately, after an hour's muddled questioning, he had managed to get his point across – and that's how we were told. Needless to say there were some heated Finnish exchanges later that night – and it was probably just as well I did not understand what was said.

Another side of being in the public eye is when people approach me wanting an autograph or just a chat. I think this public relations work is a necessary part of the job and it never worries me. Indeed, in America players are expected to do it and I think that is a good thing because it helps to promote the club and the game. It does not cost anything to be polite to people and I never find I am being pestered to the point where it becomes objectionable.

Away from football, I like going to the theatre and eating out. I also read a fair bit, especially when I am away on football trips. Nothing heavy or non-fiction though! My favourite authors are Alistair Maclean and Sidney Sheldon. But the three pillars in my life are my family, football and business interests – and I love them all.

I will miss football when I eventually have to retire because it has been good to me and has enriched my life. As one chapter closes another will open, but wherever it takes me I know it will only have been possible through my achievements with West Ham and England. I can look back and honestly say that if I could turn back the clock I would re-live it just the same.

Appendix: Career Record

Important Dates

BORN:	Barking, Essex, 1949	
SIGNED APPRENTICE FORMS:	24 July 1965	
SIGNED AS FULL PRO:	2 May 1966	
WEST HAM DEBUT:	v QPR (Chadwell Heath) W 2–1. SE Counties League Div II	5 Sep 1964
FIRST GOAL FOR WEST HAM:	v Watford (Chadwell Heath) W 2–1. SE Counties League Div II	30 Sep 1964
RESERVE TEAM DEBUT:	v Chelsea (Stamford Bridge) L 0–1. Football combination	30 Oct 1965
1ST XI DEBUT:	v Grasshoppers (Zurich) W 1–0. Friendly	8 June 1967
FOOTBALL LEAGUE DEBUT:	v Burnley (Turf Moor) D 3–3. League Div I	29 Aug 1967
FIRST GOAL FOR 1ST X 1:	v Leicester City (Upton Park) W 4–2. League Div I	26 Dec 1967
HONOURS:	Runner-up Southern Junior Floodlight Cup	1965-6
	Won Southern Junior Floodlight Cup	1966-7
	Won South-East Counties League Cup (Div I)	1966-7
	Won London Challenge Cup	1967-8
	Runner-up 'Hammer of the Year'	1967-8
	Runner-up Cagliari Youth Tournament (Italy)	1969
	First England U23 cap v Switzerland (Ipswich). Scored in 1-1 draw	1971
	Won 'Hammer of the Year'	1971-2
	Runner-up 'Hammer of the Year'	1972-3
	Full England début v Portugal (Lisbon). D 0–0	1974
	Won FA Cup	1974-5
	Runner-up European Cup Winners Cup	1975-6
	Won ITV Goal of the Season v Derby (Baseball Ground) L 1–2	1975-6
	Won 'Hammer of the Year'	1975-6 & 1976-7
	Won Prince Felippe Trophy at Santander (Spain)	1976-7
	Testimonial Match v England XI (Upton Park). Scored in 6–2 win	1977-8
	Runner-up Footballer of the Year (Football Writers Association)	1979-80
	Won FA Cup.	1979-80
	Won Football League Div II	1980-1
	Runner-up Football League Cup	1980-1
	Awarded MBE	1981

Hat-Tricks

Cray Wanderers (Chadwell Heath) 4–1 Metropolitan League	15 Oct 1966
Hatfield Town (Chadwell Heath) 5–0 Metropolitan League	14 Jan 1967
Newcastle Utd (Upton Park) 5–0 League Div I	6 Apr 1968

Away Victories

Sunderland, Leicester, Wolves, Sheff. Utd, Burnley (FA Cup), Stone (FA Cup)	1967–8
Coventry, Nottingham Forest	1968–9
Spurs	1969–70
Derby	1970–1
Crystal Palace, Spurs, Cardiff (League Cup), Leeds (League Cup)	1971–2
Chelsea, Crystal Palace, Newcastle, Everton	1972–3
Chelsea, Coventry, Ipswich, Leicester	1973–4
Burnley, Carlisle, QPR, Arsenal (FA Cup), Southampton (FA Cup), Swindon (FA Cup), Ipswich (FA Cup at Chelsea), Fulham (FA Cup at Wembley)	1974–5
Birmingham, Stone, Wolves, Bristol City (League Cup)	1975–6
Arsenal, Man. Utd, Charlton (League Cup)	1976–7
Ipswich, Leeds, Middlesbrough	1977–8
Brighton, Bristol Rovers, Luton, Newcastle	1978–9
Burnley, Cardiff, Leicester, Newcastle, Orient, Barnsley (League Cup), Everton (FA Cup at Leeds), Arsenal (FA Cup at Wembley)	1979–80
Cambridge, Chelsea, Grimsby, Orient, Shrewsbury, Swansea, Watford, Sheffield Wednesday, Burnley (League Cup)	1980–1

Appearances & Goals for West Ham United FC

Each cell is shown as **appearances / goals**. "—" indicates no appearance in that competition that season.

SEASON	FOOTBALL LEAGUE H	A	Total	FA CUP H	A	Total	FOOTBALL LEAGUE CUP H	A	Total	EUROPEAN CUP WINNERS CUP H	A	Total	OTHER 1ST XI GAMES H	A	TOTAL 1ST XI H	A	Total
1967-8	11/7	14/2	25/9	1/0	2/0	3/0	—	—	—	—	—	—	0/0	3/1	12/7	19/3	31/10
1968-9	16/5	16/2	32/7	0/0	2/0	2/0	2/1	1/1	3/2	—	—	—	0/0	13/5	18/6	32/8	50/14
1969-70	12/2	9/2	21/4	0/0	2/0	2/0	1/0	0/0	1/0	—	—	—	1/1	2/0	14/3	13/2	27/5
1970-1	10/1	9/1	19/2	—	—	—	1/0	1/0	2/0	—	—	—	0/0	5/2	10/1	16/3	26/4
1971-2	20/3	20/3	40/6	—	—	—	5/0	5/1	10/1	—	—	—	1/0	5/0	27/3	29/4	56/7
1972-3	20/8	20/3	40/11	2/1	2/0	4/1	1/0	1/0	2/0	—	—	—	0/0	10/2	23/9	33/5	56/14
1973-4	19/6	19/0	38/6	0/0	2/0	2/0	1/0	1/0	2/0	—	—	—	1/1	5/3	20/6	28/4	48/10
1974-5	18/2	18/1	36/3	2/0	6/1	8/1	1/0	2/1	3/1	—	—	—	0/0	6/4	23/2	30/7	53/9
1975-6	16/2	18/3	34/5	—	—	—	0/0	1/0	1/0	4/0	3/0	7/0	1/0	10/0	24/2	29/3	53/5
1976-7	21/2	21/2	42/4	2/0	0/0	2/0	2/1	1/0	3/1	—	—	—	1/1	5/0	24/4	29/1	53/5
1977-8	18/2	19/2	37/4	—	—	—	—	—	—	—	—	—	2/1	8/2	22/4	25/4	47/8
1978-9	11/2	10/0	21/2	2/0	1/0	3/0	1/0	1/0	2/0	—	—	—	0/0	1/2	12/2	15/2	27/4
1979-80	18/3	19/0	37/3	3/0	4/1	7/1	4/1	4/0	8/1	—	—	—	1/1	5/0	25/5	33/1	58/6
1980-1	18/6	18/4	36/10	1/0	2/0	3/0	3/0	5/0	8/0	2/0	3/0	5/0	2/0	3/0	25/6	32/4	57/10
TOTAL (1964-81)	**228/51**	**230/25**	**458/76**	**13/1**	**23/2**	**36/3**	**22/3**	**23/3**	**45/6**	**6/0**	**6/0**	**12/0**	**10/5**	**81/21**	**279/60**	**363/51**	**642/111**

Football League Record

Note: 0 = played but did not score. Total appearances 1967–81 = 458, home 228, away 230. Total goals scored 1967–81 = 76, home 51, away 25.

	DIV I											DIV II			Appearances			Goals		
	67-8	68-9	69-70	70-1	71-2	72-3	73-4	74-5	75-6	76-7	77-8	78-9	79-80	80-1	H	A	Total	H	A	Total
	H A	H A	H A	H A	H A	H A	H A	H A	H A	H A	H A	H A	H A	H A						
Arsenal	1 -	0 0	0 0	0 0	0 1	1 0	0 0	0 0	- 0	0 0	0 0	- -	- -	- -	10	9	19	2	1	3
Aston Villa	- -	- -	- -	- -	- -	- -	- -	- -	1 -	0 0	0 1	- -	1 -	- -	3	2	5	1	1	2
Birmingham City	- -	- -	- -	- -	0 0	0 -	0 0	- 1	0 0	0 0	- -	0 0	- -		6	6	12	0	1	1
Blackburn Rovers	- -	- -	- -	- -	- -	- -	- -	- -	- -	- -	- -	- -	- -	- 0	1	1	2	0	0	0
Bolton Wanderers	- -	- -	- -	- -	- -	- -	- -	- -	- -	- -	- -	- -	- -	- 1	0	1	1	0	0	0
Brighton	- -	- -	- -	- -	- -	- -	- -	- -	- -	- -	- -	- -	- -	- -	0	1	1	0	0	0
Bristol City	- -	- -	- -	- -	- -	- -	- -	- -	0 0	0 0	- -	- -	- 1	0	3	3	6	1	0	1
Bristol Rovers	- -	- -	- -	- -	- -	- -	- -	- -	- -	1 0	0 -	0 -			3	1	4	1	0	1
Burnley	- 0	2 1	1 -	0 -	- -	- -	0 0	0 1	0 0	- -	- -	- -	0 0	- -	7	6	13	3	2	5
Cambridge Utd	- -	- -	- -	- -	- -	- -	- -	- -	- -	- -	- -	0 0	0 0		2	2	4	0	0	0
Cardiff City	- -	- -	- -	- -	- -	- -	- -	- -	- -	- -	- -	0 0	- 0		1	2	3	0	0	0
Carlisle Utd	- -	- -	- -	- -	- -	- -	0 0	- -	- -	- -	- -	- -			1	1	2	0	0	0
Charlton Athletic	- -	- -	- -	- -	- -	- -	- -	- -	- -	- -	- -	0 0	- -		1	1	2	0	0	0
Chelsea	0 -	- 0	- -	0 0	0 0	0 0	0 0	0 0	- -	- 1	0 -	- 0	0 2	0	9	9	18	3	0	3
Coventry City	- -	0 1	- -	0 0	0 0	0 0	0 0	0 0	0 0	0 0	0 0	- -	- -		9	9	18	0	2	2
Crystal Palace	- -	- -	0 -	- -	0 0	2 1	- -	- -	- -	- -	- -	- -	- -		4	2	6	2	1	3
Derby County	- -	- -	0 1	1 -	1 -	0 0	0 0	0 0	1 1	0 0	0 0	- -	- 1	0	10	8	18	3	2	5
Everton	0 0	0 0	0 0	0 -	0 0	0 1	0 0	- 0	0 0	0 0	0 0	- -	- -		10	10	20	0	1	1
Fulham	2 -	- -	- -	- -	- -	- -	- -	- -	- -	- -	- 0	- -			2	0	2	2	0	2
Grimsby Town	- -	- -	- -	- -	- -	- -	- -	- -	- -	- -	- -	- -	0 0		1	1	2	0	0	0
Huddersfield Town	- -	- -	- 0	0 0	0 -	- -	- 0	0 0	- -	- -	- -	- -			1	2	3	0	0	0
Ipswich Town	- -	0 -	- 0	- -	0 0	0 0	1 0	0 0	0 0	0 0	0 0	- -			8	8	16	1	0	1
Leeds Utd	- 0	- 0	- 0	1 0	0 0	0 0	1 0	- 0	- 0	0 0	- -	- -			7	10	17	2	0	2
Leicester City	1 1	- 0	- -	0 0	0 1	0 0	0 0	0 0	0 0	- -	- 0	0 -	- -		9	9	18	1	2	3
Liverpool	- -	0 -	- 0	- 0	0 -	0 1	0 0	0 0	1 0	0 0	- -	- -			8	8	16	2	0	2
Luton Town	- -	- -	- -	- -	0 -	- -	- -	- -	- 0	- 0	0 2				2	3	5	0	2	2
Manchester City	- 0	- 0	0 -	- -	0 0	0 0	1 0	0 0	0 0	0 0	- 1	- -			7	9	16	1	1	2
Manchester Utd	0 1	0 0	- -	- 0	0 1	0 -	- 0	- 0	0 0	0 1	1 0	- -			7	8	15	1	3	4
Middlesbrough	- -	- -	- -	- -	- -	0 0	0 0	0 0	0 0	- -	- -				4	4	8	0	0	0
Millwall	- -	- -	- -	- -	- -	- -	- -	- -	- -	- -	0 0	- -			1	1	2	0	0	0
Newcastle Utd	3 0	1 0	- -	0 -	0 0	1 0	0 0	0 -	- -	0 0	- -	0 0	0 0	0 -	11	8	19	5	0	5
Norwich City	- -	- -	- -	1 0	1 0	- -	- 0	0 0	0 0	- -	- -				4	5	9	2	0	2
Notts County	- -	- -	- -	- -	- -	- -	- -	- -	0 0	0 0	0 0	0 0			3	3	6	0	0	0
Nott'm Forest	0 -	- 0	0 0	- -	1 0	- -	- -	- -	- -	0 0	- -				4	4	8	1	0	1
Oldham Athletic	- -	- -	- -	- -	- -	- -	- -	- -	0 0	0 0	0 -				3	2	5	0	0	0
Orient	- -	- -	- -	- -	- -	- -	- -	- -	1 0	0 0					2	2	4	1	0	1
Preston North End	- -	- -	- -	- -	- -	- -	- -	0 0	0 0	0 0					3	3	6	0	0	0
QPR	- -	0 0	- -	- -	- -	0 0	0 0	0 0	0 0	- 0	- -	0 0	0 0		7	8	15	0	0	0
Sheffield Utd	- 0	- -	- -	0 0	1 0	1 0	- 0	0 0	- -	- -	0 -	- -			5	6	11	2	0	2
Sheffield Wed	- 0	0 0	0 -	- -	- -	- 0	- -	- -	- -	- -	1 0				3	3	6	1	0	1
Shrewsbury Town	- -	- -	- -	- -	- -	- -	- -	- -	- -	- -	1 0	0 0			2	2	4	1	0	1
Southampton	- 0	0 -	1 0	- 0	1 1	0 0	- -	- 0	0 -	- -					5	5	10	1	2	3
Stoke City	- 0	0 -	1 -	- 0	0 0	0 -	0 1	- -	0 0	- -	1 0	- -			7	8	15	3	0	3
Sunderland	0 0	1 -	0 -	- -	- -	- -	- -	0 0	- -	0 0	0 0	- -			6	4	10	1	0	1
Swansea City	- -	- -	- -	- -	- -	- -	- -	- -	- -	- -	1 0	0 1			2	2	4	1	1	2
Tottenham Hotspur	0 -	0 0	0 0	- 0	1 0	0 0	- 0	0 1	1 1	- -	- -				9	8	17	2	2	4
Watford	- -	- -	- -	- -	- -	- -	- -	- -	- -	- -	- 0	1 0			1	2	3	1	0	1
WBA	- 0	0 0	- -	0 0	- 0	0 0	- -	- -	0 0	0 0	- -				5	7	12	0	0	0
Wolves	0 0	1 0	- 0	- -	0 0	1 0	0 0	1 0	0 0	- -	0 0	- -			8	9	17	3	0	3
Wrexham	- -	- -	- -	- -	- -	- -	- -	- -	- -	- -	- -	0 0	0		1	2	3	0	0	0
TOTAL GOALS	7 2	5 2	2 2	1 1	3 3	8 3	6 0	2 1	2 3	2 2	2 2	2 0	3 0	6 4						